Gospel Spirituality

Gospel Spirituality

by B.-M. CHEVIGNARD, O.P.

translated by Angèle Demand

SHEED AND WARD - *New York*

© Sheed and Ward, Inc., 1965

Originally published as *La Doctrine spirituelle de l'évangile*, 1958, by Editions du Cerf, Paris

Library of Congress Catalog Card Number 65-20854

Imprimi potest:
 J. Kopf, O.P.
 Vic. prov.
 Paris

Nihil obstat:
 Thomas J. Beary
 Censor Librorum

Imprimatur:
 ✠ *Robert F. Joyce*
 Bishop of Burlington
 April 8, 1965

The Nihil Obstat and Imprimatur are official declarations that a book or pamphlet is free of doctrinal or moral error. No implication is contained therein that those who have granted the Nihil Obstat and Imprimatur agree with the contents, opinions or statements expressed.

Manufactured in the United States of America

Foreword

The pages of this book were originally written for the Third Order of St. Dominic, and were published in the magazine *France Dominicaine* from 1949 to 1953. They were so well received that the author finally let himself be persuaded to publish them.

Additional chapters should have been added on the Church, the Eucharist, the Life of the Trinity, among others. However, since the author had absolutely no time available, kind readers felt that these pages could, as they were, help souls to a deeper understanding of the Gospel.

Need we say that the Gospel is not like any other book? It is the Word of God made Man. We can understand it only if we open our hearts to it completely. In this sense, the reading of these pages would be absolutely insufficient. They are intended only to be an invitation to hear the Word of the Lord and be converted by it: "Blessed are those who hear God's word and keep it."

It goes without saying that putting this accent on the Gospel does not mean that we distrust theology or the spiritual masters. The Catholic knows very well that the Christ of the Gospel can be understood only in the living tradition of the Church, with the theologians and the spiritual masters under the guidance of the magisterium. In this book, however, we wanted to rely mainly on the Gospel itself, the rich source of the Church's teaching.

Contents

Contents

viii

Gospel Spirituality

1 The Son of Man Has Come to Search Out and to Save What Was Lost

(Luke 19.10)

The first and decisive light under which a disciple of Christ should place himself, and remain his whole life, seems to be the light coming from this great word of our Lord: "The Son of Man has come to search out and to save what was lost."* By these words our Lord himself shows us what he holds in his heart for us. Let us be filled with this word. In it we shall find joy, deliverance, acknowledgement of our misery, meekness, humility, mercy for our brothers. The true Spirit of our Lord, so different from our poor wisdom, will begin to convert us.

As soon as we approach the Gospel more seriously, we cannot but be struck by the fact that Christ was misunderstood and rejected by the official holders of the religion of Israel, by the Pharisees who called themselves "just." On the other hand, he was recognized by the sinners, the publicans, actually those whom the former despised. We know whom our Lord preferred between Simon the

* The Biblical quotations used in this book are taken from *The Holy Bible*, trans. Ronald Knox. Copyright 1944, 1948 and 1950 by Sheed & Ward, Inc., New York.

Pharisee, the "just," and the repenting sinful woman. Christ knew his predilection for sinners appeared scandalous to many: "Blessed is he who does not lose confidence in me" (Luke 7.23). If he came back among us today, to which group would we spontaneously belong? Would we place ourselves with the "just" who, after all, do not need him? or with the sinners for whom he came?

We now wish to indicate the great pages of the Gospel in which Christ's love for "what was lost" is reported so movingly. Read them with new eyes. Read them once again. Remember that these words must convert us.

One day, Christ calls a man to follow him. This man is a tax collector and, therefore, not much loved. His name is Levi. He will become Saint Matthew. Before leaving, he gave a big reception in his house and invited his friends. And who were they? The Gospel says: many publicans (tax collectors, more precisely) and sinners. And we watch the Pharisees' reaction: they are scandalized. How is it possible? The Lord eats with them, the sinners and publicans!

To them we owe these amazing words of our Lord that throw so much light on his mission and show us the depths of his Heart: It is not those who are in health that have need of the physician, it is those who are sick. "I have come to call the sinners, not the just" (Mark 2.17). Hence, if men wish to hear his voice, they must know to which side they belong. Priests can testify here that they have never spoken these words, to any audience whatsoever, without a great silence following them. The characteristic accent of our Lord is heard and "his sheep recognize his Voice."

On another occasion, Christ is passing through Jericho. And there comes a man of small stature. He also is a publican, indeed a chief of publicans. Most likely his fortune was not acquired with absolute honesty. He wants to see the Lord. Out of curiosity perhaps, but also because of an obscure expectation, a need to be delivered from evil. And since he is of small stature, the Gospel mentions this picturesque detail: He climbs up into a tree, he, a person of rank in the town. He believes he is well hidden. But the Lord, when he reaches the place, simply says: "Zachaeus [he calls him by his name], make haste and come down; I am to lodge today at your house." And, says the Gospel, he came down with all haste, and gladly made him welcome, with the immense joy of a man who was at last going to live and be visited by the Lord. But there are the "just" ones, and we see the same reaction, almost the same scandal: "When they saw it, all took it amiss; he has gone in to lodge, they said, with one who is a sinner. . . ." Since there were many "just people" in town, he could have lodged with them! But let us listen to the Lord: "Today, salvation has been brought to this house . . . for the Son of Man has come to search out and to save what was lost" (Luke 19.1).

Consider with faith and love these last words, and you will find in them much light for yourself and your brothers. And the Church, with her forever surprising liturgical discoveries, has us read this Gospel at the feast of the Dedication of a Church. The holy dwelling of God is, first of all, the purified heart of a sinner.

"He has come to search out and to save what was lost." With these words of our Lord we enter into his soul. They strike the most essential fibers of Christianity: those of mercy. Here we think of the beautiful parables of the Gospel, grouped by Saint Luke in his fifteenth chapter.

In Ezechiel (Chap. 34) God spoke already as the Good Shepherd. He reproached the bad shepherd for neglecting his flock:

> Out upon Israel's shepherds, that had a flock to feed, and fed none but themselves; the milk drank, the wool wore, the fat lambs slaughtered, but pastured these sheep of mine never at all! The wasted frame went unnourished, the sick unhealed; nor bound they the broken limb, nor brought strayed sheep home, nor lost sheep found.

And, therefore, God said that he would come himself and seek his flock:

> The lost sheep I will find, the strayed sheep I will bring home again; bind up the broken limb, nourish

the wasted frame, keep the well-fed and the sturdy free from harm; they shall have a true shepherd at last.

One cannot but be struck, then, by the accent of the Gospel. It is the same accent, the very accent of God: "I will seek that which was lost." Read again now the parable of the lost sheep (Luke 15.3). How could one doubt that the Lord was conscious of coming to accomplish the Scriptures? With him, it was God in Person who came to take care of his sheep. And is it not his own accent which we perceive in these words expressing his joy, and which moves us still: "And when he does find it, he sets it on his shoulders, rejoicing, and so goes home, and calls his friends and his neighbors together: Rejoice with me, he says to them, I have found my sheep that was lost."

The parable of the lost coin with its even more striking conclusion, has the same accent: "So it is, I tell you, with the Angels of God; there is joy among them over one sinner that repents" (Luke 15.10).

But it is in the parable of the Prodigal Son that this accent is most touching. Let us simply realize that they are our Lord's own words. He spoke them. What a revelation from God, of what the Lord keeps in his Heart for the son who was lost! "But while he was still a long way off, his father saw him, and took pity on him; running up, he threw his arms round his neck and kissed him." Again, let

7

us consider each of these words; they are the words of the Lord.

In order to understand this parable fully, we must read it completely. At the beginning of his fifteenth chapter, St. Luke makes a point of telling us that he said these words for the Pharisees who were indignant: "Here is a man, they said, who entertains sinners, and eats with them." We experience constantly the same reaction. Here in the parable of the prodigal son, it is the elder son who represents the Pharisees. The attitude of his father scandalizes him and he falls into a rage: "When this son of yours has come home, one who has swallowed up his patrimony in the company of harlots, you have killed the fattened calf in his honor!" Listen to the father: "My son, you are always at my side, everything that I have is already yours; but for this merrymaking and rejoicing there was good reason; your brother here was dead, and has come to life again; was lost, and is found." It is the same accent, and even the words of "the Son of Man come to search out and to save what was lost."

Read again now the story of the repentant and forgiven sinner (Luke 7.36), that of the woman taken in adultery (John 7.53), that of Peter's denial and repentance (Luke 23.40), etc. You will always hear the same voice, and you will come to realize yourself that it is not affectivity or imagination creating a Christ for our convenience. It is the voice of the Lord himself, come to call sinners to repentance and to search out what was lost.

What shall we say? Shall we place ourselves with Simon the Pharisee who had little to be forgiven but who loved little, or with the sinful woman who loved much and had faith in her Saviour, who had come to call sinners, and therefore herself, to repentance? St. Paul, who had been a strict Pharisee respecting the law, and who might easily have become stern and fanatical, was seized by this meek and humble Lord, come for the sinners. His faith in the Saviour became the center of his doctrine. Listen to his confession, full of humility and joy, in his first letter to Timothy: "How I thank the Lord Jesus Christ, for showing confidence in me . . . a blasphemer till then, a persecutor, a man of violence, author of outrage . . ." (I Timothy 1.12 ff).

May God allow us to hear in the depth of our soul the voice of him who came to call sinners. And perhaps we shall shed the blessed tears announced by the Gospel. In any case we shall taste the marvellous fruits called peace, joy, meekness, humility, mercy for our brothers. Herein lies the first conversion suggested to us by the Gospel.

2 Christ Jesus Came into the World to Save Sinners
(I Tim. 1.15)

We have heard the Lord declare that the Son of Man has come to search out and to save what was lost. It is one of his great words, which we must always keep in our soul as our light and our joy. A lifetime will not exhaust its clarity. Let us now come back to it.

He came for sinners

Nothing sheds more light on the mystery of Christ than to know that he has come for sinners. And we do not intend here to give a subjective interpretation. Rather, we carefully accept Revelation as it is. A complete study of the Scripture is actually needed; such a study shows us the Messiah engaged in the deliverance of his people. Let us simply quote St. Paul: "Christ Jesus came into the world to save sinners" (I Tim. 1.15). One of Paul's best commentators, Ferdinand Prat, maintains that the saving of sinners was the very reason why Christ came down to earth, and that he would not have come had there been no sinners to save.*

Thus the real Christ, the only existing one, appears to us joined to our misery and our need to be saved. What a poignant revelation!

Let us repeat, this is not a subjective interpretation. Revelation shows us Christ in this light, and it is in this light that we must always see him: He came for sinners. It follows that, with regard to us, mercy appears as his major feature. And let us brush aside in this context any inconsistent insipidity. Mercy is not a pale, weak sentiment. It is a burning passion, it is Love come to share our misery and thus relieve it. The mercy of God-made-Man is poignant and infinite. It is the principle of his Incarnation and of his Cross. It is much more than an episodic aspect of his Person; it is his essential, his characteristic feature; that is what he came for. How can our sin not be submerged in his fire if with all our soul we offer ourselves to him?

Therefore, it is not our misery that can separate us from him; but the fact of our not giving it to him. And we do not give it to him, either because we do not recognize it and blindly place ourselves among the just for whom he did not come, or because we are still attached to it, or because we think that his mercy is smaller than our sin.

* Ferdinand Prat, *The Theology of St. Paul*, II (Westminster, Md.: Newman, 1946).

But if we truly give him our misery, the eagle does not fall upon his prey any faster than Christ does upon the repenting sinners that we are: "If your sins be as scarlet, they shall be made as white as snow" (Isaias 1.18).

It is in this revelation of Christ that we shall learn to know ourselves and to repent truly. And our repentance will be as a fertile valley in which the true sentiments of the Christian soul will come forth: meekness, peace, hope, mercy for our brothers. The first step has been taken and our conversion to the Gospel is coming about.

To know one's self

Guided by the light of Christ's mercy, the soul can then examine itself and become more and more aware of its misery. It is always a formidable task to descend to the inner depth of man without Christ. We know Pascal's words: "If you knew your sins, you would lose heart." From this past day, these weeks, these years, what perfectly pure gift could I make to God? How many impure and soiled things in us! St. John reports a mysterious word of our Lord telling us "that it will be for the Holy Spirit to prove the world wrong, about sin" (John 16.8). Perhaps we thought ourselves to be just, then experience came and we realized that in the depths of our heart there was much that was not pure, and we said again the verse of the psalm with a deep sincerity: "If thou, Lord, wilt keep record of our iniquities, Master, who has strength to bear it?"

But—and this is the sign of the Spirit of God—this knowledge of our fundamental impurity, instead of disturbing us, engenders great peace, because we have the knowledge of our Saviour. Our peace lies not in the evidence of our "good conscience." Who can pretend to have a good conscience? Our peace lies in the testimony of the Holy Spirit revealing to us that we are sinners, and also that Christ came for the sinners. The knowledge of man alone would soon lead us to despair or cynicism. But the knowledge of man (and the knowledge of ourselves) in the light and heart of Jesus Christ generates in us humility and peace, the true peace of Christ who teaches us that we do not have the right to despise ourselves, because he loved us in spite of everything.

Here we can speak of the blessed tears of the Gospel; not emotional and meaningless tears, but tears from the depths of our heart, the reversals and conversions which are called the humble or sorrowful regret of one's faults, compunction of heart, and, in simple terms, contrition. Those tears which our Lord blessed (Matt. 5.5), and which are a blessing indeed, are, in the Gospel, the tears of the forgiven sinful woman, the tears of Peter who denied Christ, his Master. These are visible tears, but more basically they are tears from the heart. May they also be our own tears!

*You have delivered my soul from the snare
of the fowler*

But let us really understand. We would give to Christ's
mercy a dreadful, blasphemous significance if we were to
think that he leaves us in peace with sin, that sin means
little. Sin is so serious that Christ died of it. But his mercy
becomes more apparent precisely because he really delivers
us from evil, and calls us all to be the "pure of heart who
see God."

Thus we shall experience his mercy only if from the
bottom of our heart and with a total loyalty we give him
our misery, our complete misery, so that he may cure us.
We may still be weak, we may still fall back into this
misery which we have renounced and which, nevertheless,
keeps us in chains. But our misery will not become a screen
between God and us, if we have not installed it in our
heart, if we reject it a hundred times if it attacks us a
hundred times by surprise and vanquishes us: "How often
should I forgive my brother? Will seven times be sufficient?"—"No, not seven times, but seventy-seven times
seven." Does not our Lord mean that he is always (and
always is always) close to the sinner who looks at him and
gives him, with a poor but sincere and total impulse of
faith, his misery to be purified?

It seems that once a soul has truly understood this, it
can no longer experience these long discouragements which

are so harmful. And this is, after all, not surprising. It has only begun to know what hope, true hope, is: that hope which is not built upon our own strength, but upon God's strength, immeasurable and almighty. St. Theresa of Avila once wrote: "I realize what I was in want for . . . I did not trust God completely." We realize where the crossing line is: It is in the "completely." There is a necessary self-confidence and a very dangerous self-distrust. But Christian self-distrust has nothing to do with faintheartedness. It is venturesome, daring and full of hope. It is but the reverse side of a total confidence in God. Both are co-relative: We must distrust ourselves totally in order to put ourselves totally into God's hands, and we must trust God totally in order to distrust ourselves totally. It is always a matter of faith. The Lord, after all, asks us but one question: "Do you believe in me? Do you really believe? If yes, my grace is sufficient." This profound conversion requires a whole life. But in God's name we dare to promise this: He will deliver our souls. And we can humbly sing the psalm: "O my soul, who has delivered thee? It is the Lord come to save sinners."

Blessed are the merciful

The Christian who, within himself, knows not only that he has been saved, but that he is being saved continually, how can he be so hard and despise his brothers?

St. Bernard teaches that mercy for others begins with the experience of one's own misery. "Whichever of you is free of sin shall cast the first stone at her."

We shall never pay enough attention to this: Few things are as much opposed to the spirit of Christ as an unconscious pharisaism, that creeps so easily into everything. The world is filled with it: pharisaic scandals, "virtuous" indignations, speeches on "true" justice, on "true" religion, moralizing remarks, etc. None of us can pretend to be completely free of it. We all, more or less, believe that we possess the truth, that we defend the best cause, that we are in the right camp, etc. Our Lord said sternly to his disciples: "Have nothing to do with the leaven of the pharisees, it is all hypocrisy" (Luke 12.1). Do not be afraid to descend into yourself to purge out the old leaven sticking tenaciously to wounded human nature. Or better—for in yourself you would be subtly tempted to fall into another pharisaism—open up to Christ in his meekness without thinking so much of yourself, and it is he who will take out of your heart this old leaven of the Pharisees. Then, your soul will be open to your brothers, to all your brothers, not blindly, but in the mercy of Christ. And your brothers will recognize in you, without always being able to name him, the Lord come to save sinners.

And let us have no illusions. Few things are as difficult as true mercy. As it burned in Christ, it will also burn in us. It is painful. Look at St. Dominic; he was consumed by it. He who was called the "gentle Father," would cry out at night: "What will become of the sinners?" Jordan of Saxony, his spiritual son and successor, wrote that his sense of mercy would give him no rest. And yet, it was not a bitter zeal. Of St. Dominic also it can be said "that he had come for sinners."

God is grace

What is the substance of this doctrine? The revelation of God himself. The God of the Christians, the God of our Lord Jesus Christ, the only true God, is a holy God, more holy even than almighty. His dwelling place is much less in the interstellar spaces—however astonishing they may be —than in the heart of his children. His reign is a reign of holiness. Only the pure of heart will see him. But at the same time, and no doubt because of that, this holy God comes to engulf our misery. He became incarnate, he died for the sinners. He is Grace, and he is Mercy.

What did our Lord condemn so much in the Pharisees? Was it not that they had reduced God to their dimension, to a narrow legal justice? They obeyed the law; therefore, they were "just" and the "others" were sinners. But our Lord comes to tell us that God is infinitely more: He is Grace, he is Freedom, he is Love. And we are all poor and sinners before him. Sinners and yet loved. It is from this moment on, it seems, that holiness was born on earth.

3 Unless You Become like Little Children
(Matt. 18.3)

The word of the Lord is positive: We must transform ourselves. We must become like children again, *even little children*. What an amazing word! Indeed, it has been much abused. And yet, we must receive it into our heart, let it enter into us, and let it convert us in spite of our resistance.

The conversion to evangelical childhood

Let us not be mistaken. True conversion is at stake. We know the scene of the Gospel. The disciples come to the Lord to ask him the question that bothers them: "Who is the greatest in the kingdom of heaven?" Let us not consider this trifling or childish. They want to know what is the scale of values in the new economy inaugurated by Christ. They are vaguely conscious that the Lord is bringing something really new, and they want to know, after all, what the rule will be by which everything will be judged in his kingdom. There is no doubt that the question is serious.

And we know the answer. Christ calls a child to his side,

places him in the midst of them, and says: "Believe me [that is, it is absolutely certain], unless you become like little children again [the Gospel says not only "children," but "little children"], you shall not enter the kingdom of heaven. He is the greatest in the kingdom of heaven who will abase himself like this little child" (Matt. 18.2–4).

Thus, we are forewarned. The Lord requires from us nothing less than a complete reversal of our scale of values. What matters in his kingdom, the touchstone of everything else, is the profound attitude through which man becomes little and a child again. He who attains that, is truly the greatest, the only great one in the eyes of God.

We easily grasp the depth of this conversion. Let us not call it impossible, let us not "grind our teeth," as is said in the Scripture, but let us open ourselves to the word of Christ. It will reveal to us amazing perspectives.

Blessed are the meek

One aspect of this conversion to evangelical childhood can be described as the conversion from the pride of life to the gentleness and humility of the heart.

We know the strong expression of John when he calls the pride of the world the "pomp of living" (I John 2.16). Let us look around us; almost everything is perverted by this terrible need which drives man to want the first place, the greatest authority, the greatest influence. The Christian involved in the world certainly can and must be ambitious, if by that we mean a true desire to do great things. But who does not fail to see how soon, and in what an insidious manner, this legitimate ambition is perverted through pride? Very concretely and with deep psychological insight, our Lord had noticed how much man desires what he calls "the place of honor." He had noticed it even among his disciples. With the Pharisees, it was an accepted matter. And we know his teaching: We must pass from the love of the first place to that of the last.

Here again, let us not protest. The Lord does not want to encourage faintheartedness, lack of initiative, fear of responsibility. We have, in certain cases, the duty to seek the first place or at least to hold it with authority if we have been entrusted with it. But we can readily understand where the interior conversion which Christ requires from us has its place. We must hold the first place as if it were the last; for it is in the last place that we serve our brothers and that we are sure to find Christ. Let us recall Abbé Huvelin's words: "Since Christ took the last place, we can only have the one before the last."

And it is true that he took the last place. Read again closely the scene where the sons of Zebedee ask for the place of honor (Mark 10.35; Matt. 20.20), and the answer of Christ washing the feet of his disciples (Luke 22.24; John 13.1). The washing of the feet by the Lord is not a poetical gesture without great meaning. With the Eucharist it is his testament bequeathed to us on Holy Thursday. It could not have told us more strongly what his thinking was. The true evangelical child is he who becomes the servant of his brother in such a manner "that the greatest among you be like him who serves" (Luke 22.26).

It is appropriate to recall here the beatitude of the meek (Matt. 5.4). Let us immediately rule out a certain timidity in fearful souls, without much personality. This beatitude is an extraordinary expression of strength and love. Those who attain it are far advanced in the Kingdom of Heaven. It requires the strength of love constantly at the service of one's brothers, a love which cannot be hardened either by ungratefulness, pride, bitterness, or resentment. How amazingly strong the truly meek are! Evil does not disturb them. And they understand everything. Therefore, they possess the hearts which open to them, for men know that they come not to enslave, but to serve them. We cannot but think of the Lord himself saying that he is "meek and humble of heart" (Matt. 11.29), and of his Mother called *inter omnes mitis*—meek among all. Such is the first manner of conversion to evangelical childhood.

Blessed are the poor

And here is the second conversion: we must place our strength not in perishable riches, but in the love of the Father in heaven who does not perish. The greatest man in the world is he who has the most money: accounts in the bank, various businesses, credit. How money is honored! And the Lord comes to tell us that the greatest in his eyes is he who puts his trust not in riches, but in his love; just as the dearest to us is a little child entrusted to our arms. The true child, according to the Gospel, is the poor in spirit, and the Lord has beatified him (Matt. 5.3). We cannot develop here this immense reality, underlying every page of the Gospel. Let us simply quote the following words: "Do not be afraid, you, my little flock. Your Father has determined to give you his kingdom. Sell what you have, and give alms, so providing yourselves with a purse that time cannot wear holes in, an inexhaustible treasure laid up in heaven, where no thief comes near, no moth consumes. Where your treasure-house is, there your heart is too" (Luke 12.32). We must truly become this blessed child of the Gospel again in order not to be seduced by money.

Let your word be yes for yes

The world defends its conception of greatness through lies, duplicity and pretense. What Christian never regrets being lured, in spite of himself, into a world in which almost everything is perverted? And we do not pretend that it is easy to resist. And yet, here again, we must listen to Christ: We must not resign ourselves to lying; we must

have the will to become like a child again, the disarming
child of God, as the saints were, for whom a yes was a
yes, and no a no. "Let your word be yes for yes, no for
no; whatever goes beyond this, comes of evil" (Matt.
5.37). Who does not suddenly feel that it is his truth
which passes in this clear divine word? And if we are to
be wary as serpents, we must be innocent as doves (Matt.
10.16). Again these words are the Lord's. They cannot but
have a meaning. It is truly a conversion they bring about, a
rediscovery of the true evangelical childhood they call for.

Receive the kingdom of God like a child

There is a final aspect of the conversion to the evangelical childhood, perhaps the deepest, for it closely affects
the depths of our spirit, and we can express it thus: the
conversion from the wisdom and the cleverness of the
world to the simplicity of faith. The whole story of the
Gospel shows us that the Lord was recognized, not by
those whom the world calls "clever and wise" (Péguy used
to call them "the cunning ones"), but by the little ones,
the simple and upright hearts. Faith, which means recognizing Christ in daily life, is often painful for us because
we are not simple enough. In the Church of Christ, there
is a holiness of intelligence, and we must cherish the word
of the Lord: "To love the Lord thy God with thy whole
mind" (Mark 12.30). Nevertheless, we must become

children again, in the deepest sense of the Gospel, with hearts perfectly honest and pure, profound and candid, adoring and submissive, so that the Gospel of Christ, far from scandalizing us, can reveal to us its unfathomable depths. We could quote many more words of our Lord in this context, for example, Luke 10.21. Let us merely point out the following, and reflect on them seriously: "Let the children come to me, do not keep them back; the kingdom of God belongs to such as these. The man who does not welcome the kingdom of God like a child, will never enter into it" (Mark 10.14).

We must be as open, as simple, and as candid as a child in the hands of God to receive his Kingdom, which is faith.

The essence of spiritual childhood

But what is the simple spiritual reality explaining these conversions? What is the essential attitude from which this blessed state of spiritual childhood will be born in the soul rightly and effectively? It seems to us that it is the abandonment into the hands of God and love. Here, we think, is to be found the secret of the true childhood according to Christ. Everything else proceeds from it.

The essential lesson children teach us and for which the Lord called them expressly our masters, and without which he positively warned us that we would not enter his kingdom, seems to be the following: Whereas the adult is on his guard and hardens himself, the child is trustful and open; he abandons himself to life. We must learn again with all our soul to open ourselves to God and to abandon ourselves into his hands.

Here our Lord, beyond all human reasoning and discernment, knocks at our child's heart and awakens it. His word tends to stir us, to arouse in us filial devotion. For we fortunately have in ourselves a filial stirring which his grace keeps alive and which goes deeper than human reason. Quite apart from childish sentimentality, God has given us deep spiritual instincts, supernatural instincts going beyond our reason, in which we can trust. As St. Paul says, the Spirit witnesses to our spirit that we are sons of God and has us shout: "Abba—Father." Our Lord wants to tell us here that our child's heart does not deceive us, and that in spite of the seeming incoherence of the world, in spite of the sometimes frightful aspect of life, in spite of the greatest darkness, we can trust in the child's heart which does not defend itself, but opens up to God and talks to him. It is at this moment that we have reached again the secret of evangelical childhood, and find everything simple. In fact, what God asks from us is exactly what we ask from our children: our confidence and our love. If we have truly given these to him, everything else follows: Our true richness is in God's hands, and we abhor then the lies among which the world lives, lies of pride, lies of deceit and appearance, lies of the cunning and the "wise." And we begin to rediscover our true face according to God, and to become truly new.

Unfortunately, we know that life tends to harden and close upon us. It is not a small thing to keep our true child's heart amidst the world. We even think that it requires a miracle of grace together with a deep faithfulness to God. We must, therefore, constantly look at Christ and become imbued with his Word. First of all, we must believe more deeply in his Wisdom than in the wisdom of the world.

At the beginning of this century, God granted us as a model the nun who only wished to be called "Little Sister Theresa" so as to allow everyone to become her friend. Alas, Sister Theresa was much maligned, and it is easy to understand the reaction provoked by a childish presentation of her doctrine. As a matter of fact, "Little Saint Theresa," as she is now called, is astonishingly great. But what she teaches us, who are much tempted to be despairing and cynical, is an infinite confidence in God and in the purity of love which does not look at itself.

Let us not be afraid to open ourselves to her message. It is the message of the Gospel.

Christian maturity

All that we have just said explains, we hope, how much evangelical childhood is the opposite of all affectation which has often disfigured it. We can recall Romano

Guardini's warning that the words, "If you do not become like little children," have been often misused and given a sentimental and infantile meaning. Many people have used them simply to excuse their own weakness and immaturity.*

Guardini's interpretation—so severe and so hard—seems to us to be unassailable. It is a great sorrow to see the devastations caused in every field—education, counselling, liturgy, art—by this unhealthy caricature of spiritual childhood. If we look for the origin of this alarming deviation, we find it, it seems, in the childish absence of a sense of reality. Little by little, the so-called religious life separated itself from real life and its actual conditions, to depart into the artificial, the sentimental and the childish. On the contrary, every time a Christian courageously faces life as it is, he is saved from this dangerous religious infantilism. The true remedy for this disastrous childishness consists in facing life and accepting it courageously.

If we consider evangelical childhood in its true light, we cannot but subscribe to this judgment of Guardini for whom it is the "state of Christian maturity." It is at the same time the beginning and the end, it is the door through which one enters, but also a fruit to be gathered at the end. Only the saints are perfect evangelical children. They are no supermen. They are weak and defenseless. They are children without affectation. The grace of Christ is their

* Romano Guardini, *The Lord* (Chicago: Regnery, 1954).

only richness. They have discovered their true nature as children of God. For them, their yes is truly yes, and no is no. There is no lie in them, at least no voluntary and conscious lie. They are singularly independent of the world, free and under nobody's domination. And yet, they are humble and meek, poor and pure. They are of the kingdom of Jesus. How was this accomplished? By the grace of God to which they entrusted themselves, and in which they lost themselves.

We realize now the true source of Christian strength and holiness, which establishes such a profound difference between the hero and the saint. The saint has no strength of his own; his strength is in God. He is but a child. Without any attempt at paradox, it is when he is prostrate, weak, sick, abandoned, that he is nearest to God and that he throws himself completely upon him. Read again, slowly, the extraordinary passage of the Second Epistle of St. Paul to the Corinthians: "I delight to boast of the weaknesses that humiliate me, so that the strength of Christ may enshrine itself in me. . . . My grace is enough for thee." It is when the soul experiences its humiliating weakness that it realizes that it possesses no strength of its own, but that the strength of Christ dwells in it. Then it is truly an evangelical child. The soul's strength is founded upon God's strength. And God does not fail it. The soul has reached Christian maturity.

This is your mother

To speak of the child is to evoke the mother. We have not ceased, all along, to think of Mary, Mother of Christ. Was she not, first of all, the perfect evangelical child? Let us read again her canticle, the *Magnificat;* it is the canticle of the poor, humble and gentle child, who is intrepid in her faith. Is she not also our Mother, in a special way, on this road of evangelical childhood? We have good reason to think that the Lord has entrusted to her, especially, that part of man that is childlike, that of silence and suffering. Marian souls are, in general, childlike. In the Virgin Mary, the way of evangelical childhood appears as even more simple. Is it not the road which the Child Jesus followed, he who was not ashamed to abandon himself into the hands of his Mother?

4 If Any Man Has a Mind to Come My Way, Let Him Renounce Self
(Luke 9.23)

Christ has taught us to place ourselves always among the sinners for whom he came! He also taught us that no one could enter his kingdom without becoming a little child again. And now he teaches, with the same intensity and in singularly strong terms, the necessity to renounce ourselves.

We would now simply like to evoke a few words of our Lord concerning this subject, and oblige ourselves to react to them. Only then will they speak to us.

The narrow road

"How small is the gate, how narrow the road that leads on to life!" (Matt. 7.14). The expression is striking and contains the whole doctrine: Evangelical renunciation is the narrow road that leads to life. And it is narrow indeed, but it is not a blind alley; it opens unto life immense and expanding. If the soul dares enter it, it is because it has, through grace, secretly felt that the road lead to life, the true life for which it longs.

Yet, we must not empty this word of its meaning. Our

Lord said that the road was narrow. Thus one cannot enter it with too much baggage. We must let go of many things: comfort, riches, ambitions, desire to please, all things that constitute the road that is wide and easily open to all nature. The road that leads to life is narrow, and only the resolute souls can walk on it.

It is narrow and yet it does not narrow souls. Christian experience teaches us that it expands them. Why? Because there is love. A renunciation without love does not liberate the souls, but rather it crushes them. A renunciation with love brings the soul its joy. Then the soul runs with haste on this narrow road, urged by the call of its End, by the call of Love. It senses in the depths of its own being that this is the road that leads to life.

It is always good for us, whatever state of life is ours, to question the road we have chosen. Are we walking on the wide, wide road that is easily open to nature, sinking into the ground little by little? Or are we walking on the narrow road, poor and free, urged by the call of him whom we want to reach?

At the end of her life, St. Clare of Assisi wrote these important lines in her testament: "How narrow is the road that leads to life! And likewise, how small is the gate that opens unto life! Thus, how few are those walking this road and passing through this gate! And if there are some following the way for a time, oh! how rare are those who persevere." *Lord, let me know what road I have chosen.*

Losing one's own life

"The man who tries to save his life will lose it; it is the man who loses his life for my sake and for the gospel's sake, that will save it" (Mark 8.35).

Thus it is a kind of a game where the loser wins. But one must dare lose his life, that is, dare lose his self, lose his footing, and let himself be carried away by the love of God, when so many things would hold us back.

And it is true that we must dare. We must vanquish our timidity of faith, our faintheartedness, and too human prudence. We need a kind of audacity; we sometimes even need violence. "The kingdom of heaven has opened to force; and the forceful are even making it their prize" (Matt. 11.12). We must have confidence in God to dare lose everything, to dare lose our self for him and the Gospel.

And yet, how subtly everything around us conspires to have us "keep our soul." How we fear losing our self. How we fear there will be nothing left to us. No time, no favorite occupation? No aspect of my dearly cherished and protected personality? No relaxation where I can jealously take refuge? No hidden retreat? Am I not going to keep anything at all? Yes, how difficult it is for us to "lose our life," and how, to the contrary, we want to save it with all our strength! And yet we know the word of our Lord: "He who tries to save his life [to keep it

33

jealously for himself] will lose it," but also—and we can hear in the words that follow an accent of triumph and joy—"but he who loses his life for my sake and for the Gospel's sake, he will save it." The saints are those who have lost their lives for Christ and for the Gospel.

But who will give us the strength to lose ourselves in such a manner? Another has taken us. Another must have seized us, that is to say, the Lord and the requirements of his kingdom. Thus, the same law comes back, triumphantly: It is love that explains everything and makes everything possible. Outside of love, everything is incomprehensible, impossible, complicated. Still, let but a little love and faith appear, and everything becomes possible and simple. And man really dares to lose himself.

And as he loses his self without any reservation, it happens that in fact he finds his self again, without having searched for it. And Christian experience states that this is not a word game. For man has lost a poor, narrow, fearful self in order to find again a self incomparably more true, more profound, liberated in the love for Christ and for his brothers.

Dying like the grain of wheat

Our Lord goes so far as to compare this loss of self to a death. No expression could have been stronger, and yet what an accent of triumph is perceivable in the words that follow: "Believe me when I tell you this; a grain of wheat must fall into the ground and die, or else it remains nothing more than a grain of wheat; but if it dies, then it yields rich fruit" (John 12.24).

Thus if we do not die, we shall remain alone; but if we consent to die, we shall yield rich fruit. Indeed, we must die, although we loathe death more than we think. But here death is, as it were, engulfed by life. Death is fruitful. And to the soul the promise of Christ sounds like deliverance: "If it dies, then it yields rich fruit." And what counts finally, if not to yield fruit in the vineyard of God, fruit which will endure?

To be born anew

Moreover this death, ultimately, is but the reverse side of a new birth. We must be born anew, born from God, born from the Holy Spirit (conversation with Nicodemus, John 3.3). But to be born from above, we must die to what is from below, human, too human. To be born by spiritual birth, we must die to all that is sensual in us. And how slow and difficult this death is! But what stirs us is that it is, after all, more a question of being born from God than dying to oneself. Man seized by grace is all tense in hope of his new birth. These are no longer mere words: It is true, he knows that he is being born. Then he does not see his poor human ruins in the same way: "The outward part of our nature is being worn down," says St. Paul

(II Cor. 4.17). Man knows that he is being born anew to life, through the mercy of God.

To take up one's cross

Our Lord expresses this law of renunciation in terms that have been remembered by the whole Christian tradition: We must renounce self, and take up our cross daily, and follow him (Luke 9.23).

To take up one's cross daily, is to accept everyday with courage and bravery what will crucify us during the day. It is not enough to move along and to submit to life; we must take it up and bear it. But why? Because he, the Lord, is walking in front of us: "Let any man renounce self, and take up his cross daily, and follow me." Everything that crucifies you today, heavy worries, fastidious work, numerous annoyances, all this, do not lose hold of, do not drag along. All this is valuable, for this is your cross. This is, truly, your treasure. Christ is found in it.

Any comment would weaken these strong texts. Allow us, nevertheless, to make two remarks in order to clarify them.

We wish, first of all, to recall the traditional distinction between the affective or interior detachment and the effective or exterior detachment.

The first concerns the detachment of the soul, and, here, there is an absolute. The soul cannot attach itself to anything whatever without ceasing immediately to be free to shape its course of life behind Christ. By attachment, we do not, of course, mean true love; the pure of heart love better than anybody. By attachment, we understand the concern of the soul that covets a good and sticks to it. If the soul agrees to be attached in this way, it is clear that it has agreed to slow down its course, even to halt. Here, on the interior plane of the soul's aim and its application of strength, there exists an absolute of detachment. The soul has renounced everything and is free, or it has agreed to be attached to something however little it may be—and is truly attached. There are no saints (in the world as well as in convents) who have *voluntarily* accepted to remain attached (in the sense indicated) to something. Evangelical renunciation is what gives souls their wings.

The second kind of renouncement (effective) no longer concerns the aim of the soul, but the effective use it makes of created goods. Here, there is no absolute, but only the relative which must be examined by the virtuous prudence of each man. Thus a Christian businessman must keep his heart absolutely free with reference to money (or else he does not remain a disciple of Christ), and yet he must make use of this money and even acquire some for himself and his family. His prudence must measure the use of this money according to the requirements of his love for God and his brothers, and of his responsibilities. We are here in the sphere of the relative. Yet even in this field our Lord gives his advice: "If you want to walk the narrow road you must not only be free of desires, but also you must possess few things, and at the limit you must keep nothing of your own."

The evangelical texts about renunciation are unintelligible if they are not understood interiorly in the lived flow of love. Renunciation must be placed in the positive movement of love. It is often said that renunciation is the negative aspect of Christianity. This expression is not entirely right. It is better to say, it seems, that it is the necessary reverse of love. It is a face of love. But its intimate essence is love, or else it does not exist. Without love, from which it is born, renunciation is but a concept; it begins to exist in the soul within the movement of love only. All the passages of the Gospel already quoted mention explicitly this positive and dynamic essence of renunciation: "It is the narrow road that leads to life; one must die to yield fruit; one must take up one's daily cross and follow him."

What enables the soul to take the narrow road is that it does not pay too much attention to the fact that the road is narrow, but rather that it leads to life. It is not so much a matter of taking up the cross as of choosing to love and follow Christ the Lord. So it is that the renouncement the soul feared so much, is engulfed by the impulse of love.

Do not pay too much attention to what you are to renounce, but look at the Lord with so much love that you will find that you have given up all that you feared to lose.

5 For My Sake and for the Gospel's Sake
(Mark 8.35)

We have heard the words of our Lord on renunciation. We must now find out their meaning. The question is not a useless one. It is easy to falsify its meaning, and experience teaches us that this is often done. Let us put aside, then, the false meanings of renunciation, in order to come face to face with the true one.

False meaning of evangelical renunciation

Some have tried to find in the evangelical renunciation a justification that would be horrible if it were true; they make it be a basis of resentment. The Christian would pretend to renounce violently created goods, because actually he covets them secretly. This alleged renouncement would only conceal covetousness and discontent. Such renouncement has a false intensity. Thus, to take an easy example, the woman who could not get married, belittles marriage, precisely because she wanted it; thus, elderly people often have deep resentment toward young people because the latter have a future which escapes them.

Thus, some Christians "renounce," or pretend to "renounce," because they have not truly renounced and are secretly attached to created goods.

It is clear that this interpretation of the Gospel is unjustified; it is even blasphemous. But at least it helps us to understand better the secret ties that can attach a man's heart without his knowing it. A certain "contempt" of the world really tries to hide "envy" of this world. There are bitter reformers, censors and critics who make one ill at ease. One wonders if they have really renounced what they criticize so violently. The truly detached Christian of which the Gospel speaks is "meek and humble of heart." In him we find no resentment or envy. Why should he be bitter? He has freely renounced. It is an accomplished fact. In him we see clearly that the renouncement asked for by the Gospel liberates only when it is deeply sincere. It takes years sometimes to be accepted completely. But then the soul is free: "Total and sweet resignation," as Pascal wrote.

Another deviation of the true meaning of renunciation can be fear of life. There are timorous souls who spontaneously renounce and remain in the background, much less for the sake of renouncement than because of an unconscious fear to face life. Such souls, with God's help, can ultimately regain their vigor and undertake everything for God. But there are often Christians who lack a certain vigor and magnanimity. They show a rather negative and restrictive frame of mind which leads them into a listless "material" renouncement, into an indifference which is not evangelical renouncement. Péguy described such Christians when he wrote that there are some people who think they are raising themselves into the supernatural just by debasing the natural. Then there are the too easy detachments which make us ill at ease. Any attitude marked by fear in regard to the values of the world is absolutely apart from the meaning of evangelical renouncement.

In the same line, we are all familiar with a certain canonization of failure. One consoles himself in failure by invoking the example of Christ's death on the Cross. It is very true that a certain failure on the human level can, in God's hands, become a source of graces. But one should not, therefore, fail on the human level in order to succeed on the divine level. Such failure must be an occasion of great supernatural treasures, of courage, love and steadfastness, if God is to use it in his plan.

It is easy to see the danger of these false interpretations. They reduce renouncement to something purely negative, and fail to recognize that it is valuable only if it liberates in us a higher life: God's life, and the value of charity. But if none of these are liberated, renouncement is purely and simply a failure, a poverty which is not that of the Kingdom of Heaven. Therefore, we must not be afraid to say, even to shout "from the rooftops," that such a

"renouncement," which is not evangelical, deforms souls
or else sterilizes them.

True meaning

We have already seen that the meaning of evangelical
renunciation is entirely positive. It is a road leading to life.
It moves in the direction of the positive Reality (Kingdom,
New Birth, Love of Christ), which justifies it. And if the
call to renouncement has so much appeal for the soul re-
sponding to grace, it is because it is actually the call in it
of the new life and the true love. Our Lord expressed
in his own manner, divinely and simply, this immense
Reality that expands souls. It is for him, he says, and for
the Gospel, that we are to lose our souls. His divine Person
and his Work, these are the realities which provoke and
permeate renouncement.

We can now, it seems, define this doctrine in two ways.
We can say that evangelical renunciation is the road leading to life; it is the condition of the new birth, it is the
call in us of God's great life. According to this manner of
speaking, renouncement appears more as a means of attain-
ing charity. The accent is put upon the purity necessary
in order to enter life. The beatitude of the pure of heart
refers to this kind of renouncement.

We can also say that renunciation is the proof of love,
and we can base ourselves on the phrase of the Lord: "No

one has greater love than he who gives his life for his friends." There, renouncement appears rather as the expression and the proof of charity. The accent is placed upon the generosity of love which will go as far as giving up one's life. It is the mystery of the Cross.

These two formulas cover the same reality, namely charity expressed through sacrifice, a sacrifice which liberates souls. However, the two are of such interest that we should analyze them more closely.

The road that leads to life

In order to understand the doctrine, it is indispensable that we distinguish our self according to ourselves, and our self according to God. Evangelical renunciation consists in saying no, in losing one's life, in crucifying this first self so as to liberate the second. Only on this condition is it not a mutilation and does not revolt the soul. After all, we abandon something because in one way or another we have found something more, infinitely more. Thus the merchant sells all that he has to acquire the unique pearl.

To be more precise: By the self according to ourselves, we understand:

—Our self affected by sin. Mortification does not refer to the image of God in us, but to the distortion of this image brought about through sin. One must die to sin, and not to the child of God within us. A perfectly pure heart, a world without sin, would need neither mortification nor renouncement.

—Our legitimate self, natural and human, too human even. In renouncing this self we cause the outburst of another self: the self planned by God.

By the self according to God, we understand the image of God in us, this pure heart seized by an immense and unknown love, that God wishes to create in us. This self according to God is capable of unlimited growth. It is our supernatural and Christian vocation as "saints," as "loved by God," according to the terminology of St. Paul and St. John. What profound joy to know that this "self" is not chimerical! "I believe that God loves me and that my true self loves God," said St. Francis de Sales. This true self exists in every man, just as the other self does. The carnal is real in us, but so is the spiritual, thank God! And renouncement is not the death in us of the best and the true, but their profound liberation. It is the call in us of the immense life of God. It is the "Duc in altum," "the high sea" of the Gospel, or the "call of the estuary" of St. John of the Cross.

Here the beatitude of the pure of heart has its place. Let us simply say that purity of the heart is purity of love. Purity or impurity are found in desire. If the desire is pure, the heart is pure, the eye is pure, and the whole body lies in the light. Now, the desire is pure or purified when its first impulse goes to God without dwelling upon itself. The purification effected by renouncement tends to deliver the heart, little by little, from this "retiring within itself," as wounded nature instinctively does. Theology teaches us that the fundamental wound of original sin is the dwelling of the will upon itself so as to find itself in its desires. Thus, the will no longer goes directly to God. The will clings to things because it clings to self. It is opaque. On the contrary, the Holy Virgin, in her Immaculate Conception, incarnates the beatitude of the pure of heart. She goes spontaneously to God, without retiring within her self, upright and transparent in one single impulse that lasts through all her life.

The reward promised to the pure of heart is that they will see God. Why? Because God gives himself to the humble and the pure. Moreover, because purity of the heart purifies the interior eye, and gives back to the soul its profound nature as image of God, co-naturalizes it with him, and allows it to "see" him. It is important to underline the essential tie that unites purity of heart, a consequence of evangelical renunciation, with Christian contemplation. The whole doctrine of St. John of the Cross can be put, it seems, in the light of the pure of heart who see God.

We understand better now the great positive call seen in the whole doctrine of evangelical renouncement. It is the call for a new birth and for the pure of heart. Here we have the positive good that attracts and makes possible all renouncement from within. We must lose ourselves in order to enter into life.

The proof of love

The other formula of renunciation calls upon the superabundance and generosity of charity, which tends to express itself spontaneously through sacrifice. In this light, renunciation appears more as the proof of love: "No one has greater love than he who gives his life for his friends."

Souls brought into harmony with the Christian realities by grace understand this language spontaneously. A love that would not express itself through something costly would seem a lie to them. Of course, some may go to extremes, beginners especially. The most difficult thing is not necessarily the best. Nevertheless, in today's world, completely under the sign of the Cross and the Redemption, a love without sacrifice would seem suspect. Souls must understand that a threshold must be crossed here: they must find their joy in suffering and in renouncing themselves out of love. Only then are we of the Spirit of our Lord: "There is more joy in giving than in receiving."

We notice that our Lord speaks of his Person and his Work to explain the positive reality of renouncement: "For Me and for the Gospel," says he. The demands of apostolic and missionary work create authentic renouncement by

their very nature. It is impossible to work for the Kingdom of God without losing one's life. Thus evangelical
renouncement is not practiced only in cloisters. It can be
practiced just as truthfully, sometimes more truthfully, in
a fraternal, apostolic or missionary life. The beatitude of
the pure of heart and of the generosity of love can be
realized in the very stuff of human living.

In all this, the great law of which we spoke manifests
itself more clearly. Only love, true love, is the essence of
Christian renouncement. In seeking to obtain divine love,
St. Francis of Assisi wrote the following prayer: "I beg
you, Lord, that the burning and soothing violence of your
love tear away my spirit from all things under the sky, so
that I may die of love and for your love, you who died of
love for my love."

6 *Sell All That Belongs to Thee*

(Luke 18.22)

We heard the words of the Lord on the renunciation he requires from his disciples. Let us now draw some practical conclusions.

The basic attitude is not to tolerate in the interior direction of our soul anything that could stop or even slow down our impulse toward God. We have carefully distinguished two planes: the interior plane or what the soul aims at, and the plane of exterior realization.* On the first plane no accepted hindrance to charity can be tolerated, for this would mean that the soul intends to limit charity. As to the second plane, there is no absolute but only a relative position: The actual renunciation varies with each of us. It is a matter of personal prudence which must take into account many elements, such as one's position, health, duties, etc. On the first plane, on the contrary, there is a real absolute. I must absolutely not restrict voluntarily the span of my impulse toward God.

St. John of the Cross refers to this plane when he says:

* Cf. chap. 4.

49

"It does not matter whether the soul is attached by a cable or a thread. If it is attached, it cannot fly toward God." And what keeps the soul attached? It need but accept consciously and habitually something, however small it may be, that restrains its progress toward God, and diminishes the fullness of its charity.

Let us not protest. This absolute nature of renunciation (on the plane of the interior disposition) is but the reverse of the absolute of charity: "You will love the Lord, your God, with all your heart, your soul, your strength, your mind." If I accept consciously that a part of my heart, of my soul, of my mind, be stopped by a creature, whoever it be, and be attached to it, I agree to restrict the span of my flight to God. I have broken the thrust which makes saints. The absolute of evangelical renunciation (still on the plane of the direction of the soul) is essential to the leaven of the Gospel. It must be said again and again: To accept consciously something that slows our progress toward God, is to sterilize the Gospel in us, to take from it its germ of sanctity. The salt has then become tasteless. Through our fault, the Gospel will not produce saints. And this rule is universal; it is valid for all Christians in the world as well as in cloisters.

Let us remember that such detachment does not mean a withering of the heart. The ambiguity of the expression has already been denounced. An alleged detachment from creatures which would lead us to indifference toward them

would be monstrous. Indifference is what is most fundamentally opposed to charity. We shall never love enough
nor purely enough. Evangelical renunciation tends to save
in us the ardor and the truth of love, not to extenuate us
into a bleak and icy indifference.

But we must love every creature of God, not in order
to confiscate it for ourselves, but in order to bring it back
to God. True renunciation restores wings to creatures. The
pure of heart are free and render free every creature, for
every creature's end is to be a sign of God and not a
screen or an obstacle. If it becomes a screen or an obstacle
through the fault of an impure heart, it suffers violence,
even though it may not realize it. It is captive, and it cap-
tivates. What will restore its wings, except purity of heart?

Thus, if I realize that a creature, whatever it may be—
woman, child, profession, culture, art, beauty—halts and
restrains my impulse toward God and toward the fullness
of charity, I must conclude that my heart is not yet pure
enough. I do not yet love with the strength and the truth
that evangelical renunciation will teach me. I am not to
cease to love; I must love better, I must love much more.
And all things will begin to exult for me as they never
did exult.

This purity of heart that does not cleave to any creature is, first of all, the work of the grace of God operating
through charity. We are asked to be always open to this
grace in the expectation of an ever more profound and

liberating purification. At certain times, God may effect a tearing-up: "If your eye is an occasion for falling into sin, pluck it out." It may require the tearing-up of one's heart, of one's spirit. But if the soul is faithful, if it has let itself be captivated by God, the work of grace will detach it progressively—with care and strength—from all its unconscious attachments. And the beatitude of the pure of heart will appear to it like a great universe of light and peace, which grace invites it to enter.

Thus we must always, with jealous care, maintain intact in us the purity of the interior aim of our love. This is the first zone, the deepest one, of evangelical renunciation. The soul must always be ready to put aside, out of love, whatever God will ask it to put aside.

Can we, however, formulate some rules with reference to the exterior and concrete realization of renunciation?

The first will consist in accepting without cheating and with all our love the real life God sends us every day.

Renunciation comes with real life. We need not look for it with self-imposed privations. It comes to us in a much deeper manner. We have but to accept our complete life and let no part of it become lost. Open your eyes. Almost at every minute renunciation is proposed to you by that which actually makes your life. And in a very special way, through the complete acceptance of your responsibilities and the exigencies of fraternal charity.

Our responsibilities are varied, multiple, profound. We must weigh them seriously. At no price must we evade them. And often it takes great courage to face them. Children to feed and bring up, workers to supervise, elderly parents to take care of, daily tasks to perform; it is by offering myself to these responsibilities with all my heart, my mind and my strength that I shall accomplish the renunciation God asks of me. And if I put love into it, the law of the Gospel is fulfilled: renunciation becomes inseparable from love, and it is as if it were absorbed in the movement of love.

Love for our brothers will also bring us our daily share of renunciation. To offer oneself to fraternal charity is necessarily to offer oneself to renunciation. There are few things that force us to die to ourselves as surely as fraternal charity. Again, open your eyes, and see in your life this brother of Christ weighing upon you. Do not go out of your way to find renunciation. Accept this brother, but accept him truly and you will permanently have in your life a source of renouncement. And you can be sure that this will be true renouncement. It comes from Christ and sanctifies you. On the other hand, if you avoid your brothers, mortify yourself as you may, you will have missed the essential. You will not have died to yourself. How good God is to have thus placed in our lives ways of finding him at all times.

Must we go further? Must we impose on ourselves privation of what we rightly enjoy? Most certainly, but we must do it with a free spirit and with joy. The more care we take to keep our heart pure and to open ourselves to our responsibilities and our brothers, the more freedom we shall have in this area.

We could find further inspiration from the Church. Liturgical life gives us quite naturally the very web of voluntary renouncement. There are definite times for prayer and penance. Could we not, even in small things (delay smoking a cigarette, not have a coffee break today) show God that we are docile to his spirit? What is important is to do it with joy and almost unconsciously: "God loves him who gives with joy," says St. Paul.

There remains the fact that God himself directs our lives. And in his wisdom, he always associates us more or less to the mystery of the Cross of his Son. There are renouncements that only God can effect, and that concern in each soul precisely that which needs to be purified. The life of Christians is a living proof of it. "How God has purified me little by little," they love to say at the end of their life. Weak health, loss of loved ones, solitude, great worries, these are ways in which God leads his friends along the way.

This is where fidelity to grace, the living law of Christian renouncement, comes in. We need not overtake grace and imagine that God asks from us what he may never ask for; we must, with much more humility, follow grace, without scruples and agitation, but faithfully and simply. To this end we must abandon ourselves, in a filial way, to God. We must not doubt God, but be sure that he will not deceive us.

Thus God induces us, little by little, to lose our soul. At that moment, we shall begin to know the true meaning of freedom.

7 Why Didst Thou Hesitate, Man of Little Faith?

(Matt. 14.31)

All the exigencies of the Gospel are understandable through faith only: living faith in the living Person of Christ. All we said about conversion of the heart, about evangelical childhood, about renunciation, can only be explained in the movement of faith. The Lord, after all, asks us but one question: "Do you believe in Me?" And living faith in his Person brings about everything else.*

Now, we find two aspects of this faith in the Gospel. To believe means, on the one hand, not to doubt God, to depend on him with intrepidity amidst the worst hardships; thus, the Apostles should not have been fearful on the boat as the storm arose (Mark 4.35). On the other hand, to believe is to recognize Christ interiorly. Thus Peter recognized him as the Messiah and the Son of God in Caesarea Philippi. In the first instance, the emphasis is put on total confidence; in the second, it is put on knowledge. Confidence and knowledge, far from opposing one other,

---

* In the following pages we are always speaking of the "living" faith. We do not deny, however, that faith without charity already represents an invaluable benefit.

57

complement each other and form the total living faith. For how could we trust in him whom we have not recognized? And could we say that we recognized him if we did not trust him completely? We shall now try to clarify these two aspects.

It is practically impossible to understand the faith required by Christ without going back to the Old Testament. The essential religious attitude Christ asks from his people from the Old Law on, is an attitude of faith in him. We need only read chapter eleven from the Epistle to the Hebrews where the author gives us, as examples of faith, all the saints of the "Old Alliance."

Rely upon God who does not yield

Nothing is more enlightening than the study of the Hebrew word expressing the attitude of faith. There is no equivalent of the word "faith" in this language. It is the verb that exists, the verb expressing not only a concept, but an entire attitude. Now, the Hebrew verb "aman," which is used to express the attitude of the man who has faith, can also be translated: to rely upon someone who does not yield.* That is what God asks from man in the first place.

* Whence the expression often used: "God is my rock." Cf. also the theme of the "cornerstone" in the Gospel and the name "Peter" given to Simon.

The same verb can also be translated: to let oneself be carried, be fed by someone. Here again, what a revelation! To have faith in God is to let him carry us, feed us.* The whole revelation of the Good Shepherd and of the Father in Heaven is already germinating in this word.

He, upon whom we can thus depend, and by whom we can let ourselves be carried, is then called "faithful." This admirable word is almost reserved to God. He is called "God, faithful to all his promises," and Christ will be the "faithful witness." What does this mean? Amidst this world in which everything gives way, amidst this world in which we find so many lies, you can depend upon God: He does not deceive amidst this world in which the best people are so changeable. You can rely upon God: He is faithful. That is to have faith, according to Scripture.

Our Lord uses the same term in the expression: *Amen, amen, dico vobis.* The word "Amen" is, in fact, the adverb formed from the verb "aman," expressing faith. Therefore, when our Lord uses this expression, he appeals to our faith, and somehow he binds himself: "I tell you, I promise you, you have only to believe me." Read again some of the great promises of Christ beginning with these words, and you will feel their authority (Mark 10.29; 11.23; Matt. 18.3).

* Cf., for example, Numbers 11.2, the complaint of Moses to God that it was not he who brought the Jewish people into the world. Why should he carry them on his back and nurse them in his bosom? The verb "aman" is used here.

What is striking, almost baffling, is the absoluteness that God requires in faith, since the time of the Old Testament. Moses doubts in his heart, for one instant, before striking the rock from which the living water is to flow in the middle of the calcinated desert. And because he doubted, he was not to see the Promised Land. And who among us would not have hesitated? "One must not doubt in one's heart," says our Lord (Mark 11.23). It is clear that this quality of absolute faith bears a divine stamp. No man, however loved, can require such faith from another; he is but a fragile man. But God, he can require such faith from us.

The great figure, in this connection, towering over the Old Testament, is evidently Abraham. If we read his story we find a man a hundred years old, and his wife close to the same age. They have no children. Everything is finished for them. And yet, God says to him: "Look at the sky, count the stars if you can, such will be your posterity." And St. Paul goes on: "There was no wavering in his faith; he gave no thought to the want of life in his own body, nor to the deadness of Sarah's womb" (Rom. 4.19). It is this quality of faith that God requires. The man who has such belief has found a rock in his life. And nothing can glorify God more.

It is the same type of faith that our Lord requires in the Gospel. He requires such faith in God, but how extraordinary! he requires it for himself, thus underlining his divine origin and nature: "As you have faith in God, have faith in me" (John 14.1), the same total and absolute faith.

Walking over the water

We must admit that the Gospel confounds us, for our Lord quietly asks that we do astonishing things, such as walking on the water and moving mountains. We know well these scenes of the Gospel.

He comes to his disciples walking on the sea (Matt. 14.25). And upon his word, Peter does not doubt. He lets himself out of the ship and walks over the water. "Then, seeing how strong the wind was, he lost courage and began to sink." We rather understand his fear. Walking over the water, Lord, after all, is not natural for a man. And yet what does the Lord say? Jesus stretched out his hand, caught hold of him, and then said: "Why did you hesitate, man of little faith?" These simple words have such great meaning for us. Thus, what you ask from us, Lord, is not to doubt your word, even when we are walking over water. We find the same lesson in the calming of the storm (Mark 4.35), and in the healing of the possessed child (Mark 9.14), the daughter of the Chanaanite woman (Matt. 15.21), and the centurion's servant (Matt. 8.5). Read these Gospels, and read them again. Through them the Lord talks to us directly and continually. He asks us the same question. "Do you believe in me in this way?" That is, with absolute unconditional faith, which is, so to speak, the proof that we treat him as God. It is the sign that we have found him. Then, we have a God, the true and only God. Then, if we had faith, though it be like a grain of mustard seed (Matt. 17.19), we would only have to say to a mountain, for example: move from this place to that, and it would move. *Lord, give us this grain of mustard seed.*

Such faith grows amidst the trials of life. The Gospel does not cultivate souls in hothouses. We could say that it is a book for high winds, the high wind of God, to serve as resistance against the high wind of the world and of evil. Now, it is in the wind of life that our faith is tried. How silent God remains sometimes! How he remains in a state of sleep! Why do the wicked triumph? It is often in life that we have to walk over the water, that we have to move mountains, the heavy mountains of prejudice, of habit and human vulgarity. Then the Lord simply repeats these same words: "Why did you doubt, man of little faith?"

Your sins are forgiven

The same faith is required for the forgiveness of sins. We know that it is a greater miracle to give a withered heart life again than to cure a palsied man (Mark 2.1). And yet, Christ affirms in the Gospel that he grants this miracle to faith.

"Do you believe in Me?" he asks the sinner. What does it mean? Have you enough faith to lose yourself in me? It is not in you that justice and sanctity are found, but in me. You must leave yourself, your small and narrow justice, you must lose yourself in me. Such faith includes, of course, the voluntary and radical detachment from sin, but the soul also ceases to look for salvation in itself. It understands that its purification must be much deeper. Another must take care of it. Another on whom it can cast itself, divided yet, with all its poor faith and its poor love. At certain times, it will only be able to flee to him, shout for him. And his Person will purify it from sin. We know that St. Paul made faith one of the turning points of his doctrine.

Thus, the woman who was a sinner comes forward and falls at his feet and cries. She has found her Saviour. Her heart receives life again, and it becomes truly new. A miracle has happened, greater than when water gushed forth from the rock. Why? Because she has believed. She believed in Christ who had foretold her. The Lord simply said to her: "Your faith has saved you" (Luke 8.48).

The priests of Christ today attest that the Gospel continues. The victor of sin is faith in Christ.

Follow me

The Lord, then, can ask for anything. Read again the passages of the Gospel where his requirements are so strong.* The same law bursts out everywhere: It is faith that makes everything possible. Faith in his Person carries off everything in its living flow. And man leaves his house, his field, his family, and, above all, he leaves himself, because he has faith in him. But if his faith dies out, everything stops, becomes dead, and the Gospel is but a mass of obligations, impossible to understand and even less to fulfill.

What is necessary in order to receive this priceless treasure of faith? Our Lord tells us himself, we must become humble like a child: "The man who does not welcome the kingdom of God like a child, will never enter into it" (Mark 10.15). For faith is a gift. It must be begged for, desired, searched for, waited for patiently. And once the first germ is received, one must have the courage to go ahead. Faith, then, requires the generosity of a child who does not calculate. It requires souls who know how to give of themselves. And that is, no doubt, why God asks for it with so much insistence. We must dare lose ourselves by trusting God totally.

Faith is at the beginning only like a grain of mustard seed, but then it grows and spreads over all the earth.

* For example, Luke 9.23–26; 12.51–53; 14.25–29, etc.

8 And You, Who Do You Say I Am?
(Matt. 16.15)

To believe in Christ is to depend on him fearlessly and not doubt him, even when walking over water, or facing mountains to be moved. But what makes possible this impulse toward him out of the depth of a being? It is because God has mysteriously made himself known to us. He gave us his light. To believe is to recognize Christ interiorly.

To recognize Christ

Already in the Old Testament this characteristic of recognizing God is marked. No doubt, to believe in Yahweh is to depend on him in one's heart, even through the worst trials of life. But is this a blind instinct? No, surely not. For God has enlightened man. He has made known that he is here, alive. In this sense, according to the mysterious and striking expression of Isaiah, to believe is to "understand that it is he," to understand it with a mysterious and complete certitude. "You are my witness . . . so that you will recognize me, and believe me and understand that it is I" (Isaiah 43.10).

Gospel Spirituality

This aspect is even more emphasized in the Gospel. The whole story of the Gospel can be summed up as the story of the recognition of Christ. And we can say that today still the mystery of the Gospel and of the Church in the world is this same mystery of the interior recognition of Christ through faith. The question the Lord asked Peter, he does not cease to ask us in the depth of our soul: "And you, who do you say I am?"

This is no illuminism; we are simply at the heart of Christian faith. Faith is more than a simple intellectual adhesion to revealed truths. It is Christ's revelation itself. More even than revealed truths, it is God revealing himself. Open the holy Bible; from beginning to end it is the Book of God who reveals himself. Open the Gospel; from beginning to end it is the revelation of Christ. We can say in all truth that the light of faith shines, first of all, upon the very Person of the Son of God and consequently upon the truths that he has revealed. Then faith is living, for it is a living Person that we have found at the very heart of our life. We cannot be overwhelmed enough in adoration of this mystery, and in the humble and imploring expectation of his coming.

Certain great scenes of the Gospel persuade us that we face here the essential of our faith. The Lord is sitting down by the well, like a simple foreigner. A woman comes to draw water. So far they are two strangers to each other, at least so it seems. This woman has a life of her own. She

66

is carefree. She is far from thinking that in a few minutes everything will be changed for her. The Lord speaks first, to ask for a service: "Give me some water to drink." And the conversation begins. Immediately he goes straight to her soul: "If you knew what it is God gives, and who this is saying to you, give me to drink, it would have been for you to ask him, instead, and he would have given you living water" (John 4.10). What is this living water, bringing everlasting life to the soul? It is the faith. But what is faith? Faith is Christ, but it is Christ living, actually communicating to the depth of the soul: "I, Jesus said, who speak to you, am Christ" (John 4.26). And the woman put down her pitcher of water, and went back to the city. She had forgotten what she had come for. Her mind was filled with other things. She had found Christ, in the very heart of her life.

The man who had been born blind was cast out from the synagogue (John 11.35). His cure is embarrassing for those who do not want to see. He finds Jesus. And the Lord simply asks him: "Do you believe in the Son of Man?" And he, with his ardent and forthright soul, says: "Tell me who he is Lord, so that I can believe in him." Jesus answers: "It is he who is speaking to you." And the man fell to the ground prostrate, and with his soul dazzled and adoring, he said: "I do believe, Lord."

We could relate many more such incidents from the Gospel. The same mystery bursts out everywhere: a man recognizes Christ and Christ is no longer a stranger to him. He enters into the heart of his life. The Lord, finally, asks always the same question: "And you, who do you say I am?" And if we can answer with Peter: "You are Christ, the Son of the Blessed," then we have found him. Again, here is the essence of our Christian faith. As much as we may speak about mysterious realities, as long as faith does not first concern itself with the Person of Jesus, we do not possess faith in its full mystery. We may know a set of well-connected truths (and this is necessary) or a tradition (necessary also), yet we shall not have the faith Christ requires from us. Let us say it again, for every Christian, even a businessman in the grip of a terribly relentless life, he has faith only if the Person of Jesus is at the heart of his life. And this is nothing sentimental, but only a deep and supernatural faith. Then everything becomes clear; religious practice begins to live and the Gospel speaks. Everything is simple. But if the Person of Jesus is absent, everything becomes dead, everything becomes complicated. How we would wish to tell souls that this is faith: to have the Person of Jesus living in one's life.

To be born of God

Let us not believe that sensitivity or even intelligence are sufficient to have faith. Faith is a mystery. All supernatural faith in a man is a mystery by which God intervenes constantly. Listen to the Gospel. Peter recognized Christ. And the Lord calls him blessed; yes, blessed "because it is not flesh and blood, it is my Father in heaven that has revealed this to you" (Matt. 16.15). Thus this interior recognition of Christ is not the order of flesh and blood (sensitivity, natural intelligence, historical, psychological or artistic intuition, etc.). We must go beyond the whole world. Faith is of another order, beyond all created order. Faith is the revelation of his Son that the Father gives us. Through faith, we leave the order of human generations; we have part in the generation of God himself. St. John, always so forceful in expression, speaks of a new birth. Through faith, we are born from God himself, and that is why faith in its utmost mystery escapes all human investigation. Each of us who believes is a great mystery; our birth came "not from human stock, not from nature's will or man's, but from God" (John 1.13). For us also, "God saw fit to make his Son known in us" (Galatians 1.16). God saw fit! In our faith we are dependent upon the benevolence of his Love. And he wishes us to know it and to find therein our joy.

Does this mean that no human preparation is necessary? To think so would be to ignore the wisdom of God which unites all things together, the natural and the supernatural, long preparations and sudden eruptions of his grace.

At the outset, he asks for and arouses a forthright and humble heart: "We must receive the Kingdom—which is

living faith—like a child" (Mark 10.15). It is the heart of
the centurion, of the Chanaanite, of the man born blind. It
is the heart of the shepherds at the crib, of Zacharias, of
Elizabeth. It is the heart of Peter, of John, and of Paul.
Still more elevated, it is the heart of Mary, his Mother. It
takes such a childlike heart to receive the Gospel and to be
in harmony with the wisdom of God, "who has hidden
all this from the wise and the prudent and revealed it to
little children" (Luke 10.21). One cannot cease, or even
begin, to become like a child, in the holy sense of the
Gospel. What is needed, is a heart amazingly open to God,
serious and candid, knowing that nothing is impossible to
God; a heart ignoring itself; a generous heart able to give
without return; a faithful heart, fearless in the face of its
adversary.

Such humble and upright hearts see the signs of God. For
God gives signs. He has pity on our unknowing. He does
not scorn our legitimate urgency to know. He knows that
he created us spirits made for the truth. He does not give
signs to the proud who put him to questioning, nor does he
give signs to souls still impure, more in quest of wonders
than of faith. But he is pleased to give signs to the man
who, with all his eager and often desolate heart, searches
for him gropingly. He gave signs in the Gospel. He still
gives signs today. Some are valid for his whole Church; the
time for miracles is not completed. Some are valid for him
only who receives them: relief of pain, a period of quiet, a

friendly heart, a child's smile, a soft light in someone's eyes and, above all, the irresistible and mysterious attraction of the saints. It is in them that Christ reveals himself most; humble and true saints whom we cannot doubt because we see their lives. These are the signs of God supporting the faith of his children walking toward him.

But all this is living only if the Father in Heaven is part of it. When for the first time we stammered our faith, he was here. He wrapped us in his light. And there is the testimony of his Holy Spirit to our own spirit (Rom. 8.16). We must no longer delay; we must let ourselves be taken by God and taught by his Church. We must dare to believe. And what do we believe? That Jesus is living and that the whole Christian mystery is true. And that our poor world does not go toward a dark night, but toward the radiant City of God.

Christ is hidden in God

When we read the Gospel, we find that this gift of God, which faith is, is presented mostly in terms of light and revelation, and not of night and desert. It is the living water Christ promised us, and not the aridity of the dried-out earth: "If a man believes in me, fountains of living water shall flow from his bosom" (John 7.38). Faith is a light before being a night.

Yet, there is in the Holy Books a long experience of the

desert and of the absence of God. There are the complaints
of Job. Above all, there is the cry of the Lord on the Cross:
"My God, my God, why have you forsaken me?" Can we
still speak of light and of the interior revelation of Christ?

And we say: yes. For in order to be known in his full
mystery, Christ cannot be known only in the joy of his
light. We must know him also in the agony of his holy
soul and in his abandonment upon the Cross. In one word,
we must know him crucified. What a lesson the Gospel
teaches us here! It is immediately after the profession of
faith of Peter that the Lord "began to make it known to
them that the Son of Man must be much ill-used"
(Mark 8.31). And we know that it took the apostles a
long time, though they had recognized the Lord in their
faith, to recognize and accept him in his Cross. Here begins
a new revelation of Christ, a state of faith even dearer to
God. Listen to St. Paul: "Him I would burn to know, and
the virtue of his resurrection, and what it means to share his
sufferings, moulded into the pattern of his death, in the
hope of achieving resurrection from the dead" (Phil. 3.10).
We can know Christ only if we are in conformity with
him in death.

And after the Ascension, he disappeared. "It is better for
you I should go away" (John 16.7). Our faith must rise
anew: "You must lift your thoughts above; you must be
heavenly-minded, not earthly-minded" (Col. 3.1). "Your
life is hidden away now with Christ in God" (Col. 3.3).

Where is Christ now? He is hidden in God, even when we receive him in the Eucharist. Our faith must still be purified: "Henceforward, we do not think of anybody in a merely human fashion; even if we used to think of Christ in a human fashion, we do no longer" (Cor. 5.16). What counts is not to be consoled, but that God's will be done in us and in the world. Yet it is always Christ that our faith seizes more and more deeply. And God seems to remain silent. And the wicked triumph. And this world appears to be without soul and without sense. And the ungodly ask us: "Where is your God?" And in our innermost being we know that he is not far away, and that he is this same Christ dead, crucified, abandoned to the hands of man, but resurrected on the third day and now hidden at the right hand of his Father.

All this was contained in his question: "And you, who do you say I am?"

9 My Meat Is to Do
the Will of Him Who Sent Me

(John 4.34)

Through living faith, the central reality of the Gospel, we know the divine Person of Jesus. Faith is the unique sap of the soul; without faith all religious practice is but dead wood. Yet we are so weak that we can egotistically take pleasure in ourselves over so great a reality. This is why the Gospel leads our efforts towards an attitude that allows no illusion, and that our Lord calls "doing the will of his Father." This is the mark of true love. This is the sign of the true disciple of Jesus Christ.

*He is my brother ... who does the will of
my Father who is in heaven*

We know this great moment in the Gospel (Matt. 12.46). Someone told the Lord that his brethren and his mother were looking for him. But he made this astonishing answer: "Who is a mother, who are brethren, to me?" Then he looked about at his disciples who were sitting around him, and stretching out his hand toward them he said slowly: "Here are my mother and my brethren! If

75

anyone does the will of God, he is my brother, and sister, and mother."

Once more, let us consider these meaningful words and let them enter our soul. Thus our Lord tells us in the clearest possible manner who is close to him, who is dear to him, who belongs to his family and, to use these same strong words, who is "his brother and his sister and his mother." We would never have dared use such words. Thus we can be his brother, his sister, his mother. Let us receive these words with adoration and love.

Let us receive them also with awe, the religious awe that tolerates no illusion. For it is neither transports of feeling, nor great enthusiasm, nor even interior light, that make us agreeable to God. All this can be grace, but it can also be impure if we linger over it. We must go further and build upon the rock: "The Kingdom of Heaven will not give entrance to every man who calls me Master, Master; only to the man that does the will of my Father who is in heaven" (Matt. 7.21).

Lord, preserve us from illusion and let us be found truthful in your love.

My meat is to do the will of him who sent me

And why does the Lord call him who does the will of the Father in Heaven his brother, his sister and his mother?

Because he was himself consumed with this passion to do the will of his Father, and because he truly recognized as his own whoever would share this same passion. In St. John there is a saying of his in this regard, that we must often mediate in our heart: "My meat is to do the will of him who sent me and accomplish the task he gave me" (John 4.34).

It has been rightly remarked how little our Lord said about himself. Yet, he thought it fitting to give us a few words which are like flashes of light upon his holy soul. And so he tells us that he is "gentle and humble of heart" (Matt. 11.29); that he has "come to spread fire over the earth, and what better wish can he have than that it should be kindled" (Luke 12.49). Here he reveals to us what is his innermost nourishment and the secret of his being: to do the will of him who sent him.

Every soul has its food; every soul searches for its food. It is an important matter to know what nourishes the soul. There are foods which, though good, are simply earthly; they satisfy a certain hunger, but they suffocate higher needs. There are weak foods which nourish weak souls. And then there are strong meats which nourish strong souls. To do God's will is a nourishment of the latter kind.

When the soul is tired and weary, it searches for a drink of living water. It searches for it on earth, and the earth does not give it any. It searches for it in heaven and heaven remains closed. And yet, if it can go deep enough within itself, it finds profound peace in desiring only the will of God. Here is its essential need; here it finds its deepest nourishment. Let us ask God for this hunger; let us ask him to be satisfied only with this food. *O my soul, what is your hunger, and what is your meat?* Is it to desire only that God's will be done? And not only that it be done, but that you do it?

Thy will be done

We know where this hunger led our Lord: to Gethsemane and to the Cross. We have kept the prayer he made when he fell upon his face: "My Father, if it is possible, let this chalice pass me by; only as thy will is, not as mine is" (Matt. 26.39).

True love is not found in emotional outbursts or in ecstasy; it is found in loving the will of God more dearly than our own, however crucifying his will for us may be. The true friends of Christ feel it instinctively. All other food seems tasteless to them. In time of distress, they humbly repeat in their heart the words of Christ: "Only as thy will is, not as mine is." Or, from the depths of their soul, they say over and over, as their most intimate and dearest aspiration, the same prayer of the Saviour: "Yes, that all thy will be done in me and in the world."

The Father is always with me

The secret of this profound attitude can only be in love. It is more than external, ever ready, obedience. There must be love. There must be the presence of God. Our Lord reveals to us that "I am not alone, because the Father is with me" (John 16.32).

The Father is always with him, because he always does "what pleases him." God is always with the soul who prefers his will to its own. He is with it more certainly, therefore, than in time of consolation. It is this presence of God, this presence of Christ, which is the supreme nourishment of the soul who seeks only his holy will, and who is in accord with it.

Let us meditate on this divine revelation. The words of the Lord teach us, first of all, the Truth of Love. It is not easy to know if one loves truly. Our Lord tells us clearly: "He loves who prefers the will of God to his own and whose meat it is."

But these words would be arid if we took them to mean only an external, formal obedience. Then "to do God's will" would be but a mere formalism. It must be understood that love addresses itself first of all to a person. Christian life has at its center the divine Person of Jesus. If we do his will, it is because we love his Person. "To do the will of God" can be understood only as the impulse of love going to the Person.

It remains true, then, that the only true love is the love that takes for its nourishment the holy will of God. Every other "love" is certainly suspect. How can we read the Gospel without being struck by this truth, by this profound respect which emanates from the words of our Lord when he speaks about his Father? What strength and what purity! Indeed he tells us to love God with all our strength, with all our heart. But what does this mean, if not that his will must conquer us and become our law and our most intimate food?

At this point, true love has plunged its roots into the soul. To repeat, raptures can be deceiving, but there is no deception in the loving performance of God's will day by day. The soul who does God's will at every instant finds in this its quiet nourishment and lives in the truth. Even if it does not have many graces of light, our Lord calls it "his brother and his sister and his mother."

Docility to the ways of God can be the second meaning found in these great words of our Lord. What matters is not to find an extraordinary way, but to love the way God intends for us, to be perfectly docile in his hands.

Our daily experience with souls reveals what is perhaps the most difficult thing for them: the perfect abandonment to God's guidance. Many grow tense, defend themselves, distrust God unconsciously: They do not "lose their footing." It seems to them that they will lose themselves if they abandon themselves truly to God. And in fact, they will lose themselves, but if they dare to lose themselves truly, they will finally be his children, his true children with whom he can do what he wishes. Other souls want to do things too well, they are always ahead of God; they do not yet know how to follow him; neither holding back, nor rushing headlong. Both have failed to understand that God's ways are not our ways, and that to abandon oneself truly to his will is to enter an infinite universe so much more admirable, more marvellous than that of our poor, still too human, desires. "See how well I led the holy Virgin and the saints," Pascal has the Lord say. Another time, in St. John, Christ says to Nicodemus: "The wind breathes where it will, and thou canst hear the sound of it, but knowest nothing of the way it came or the way it goes; so it is, when a man is born by the breath of the Spirit" (John 3.8).

He who is truly abandoned to the will of the Father in Heaven is carried away by the breath of the Spirit. Like Theresa of Lisieux, who was proclaimed universal patron of the Missions, he may spend his life doing things which the world calls small, and yet he will be great in God's eyes. And he may do things which the world calls great and which are great indeed, and yet he may have done them without knowing that God did them in him.

Finally, this very holy will of God, more dearly loved than our own, teaches us about the very nature of God. The God of the Gospel, the one true God revealed, is a

Father who leads his children. He is not a mere object of contemplation in the static sense of the word. He is supremely active. He is holy and he is free. Therefore, our holiness cannot but consist in going with him. A simple attitude of spiritual admiration is not sufficient. We must become involved. We must cooperate with his fatherly will, which never ceases to move us in our innermost self. Sometimes, his ways are baffling; they scandalize our human wisdom. With Jesus, we can repeat his cry from the Cross: "My God, my God, why has thou forsaken me?" But with Jesus our fears will always be allayed, and we can say that final word that he wanted to give us as the supreme lesson of his life and teaching: "Father, into thy hands I commend my spirit." Then can we truly be called by him: his brother, and his sister, and his mother.

10 Our Father, Who Art in Heaven
(Matt. 6.9)

Living faith in Jesus is, as we said, the living soul of the Gospel. His divine Person is the center of our faith. But he himself directs our eyes toward Another whom he calls his Father and whom he has us also call "Our Father."

He is moved to compassion

The Christian generation of today—at least its elite—seems to understand better the unity of the holy Bible. Thus they understand that the Gospel must be read in the light of the Old Testament. While Christians underline the truly new and transcendent character of the Gospel when compared to the Old Testament, they love to acknowledge, nevertheless, the marvellous continuity between the two testaments.

The same applies to the revelation of God to the Father. Our Lord speaks of the Father with a unique accent; there is no doubt that in revealing himself as the only Son, he gives to this Paternity a sense we could not otherwise know. And yet, even in the Old Testament, this deep vein

83

of revelation is opened, and our Christian soul can recognize with emotion the very accent of Christ in certain passages of the prophets.

Read, for instance, Osee (11.1–9), the prophet of mercy:

Israel in his boyhood, what love I bore him! Away from Egypt I beckoned him, henceforth my son. . . .

They called them, the more they refused obedience; gods of the country-side must have their victims, dumb idols their incense! Yet it was I, none other, guided those first steps of theirs, and took them in my arms, and healed, all unobserved, their injuries. Sons of Adam, they should be drawn with leading-strings of love; never waggoner was at more pains to ease bridle on jaw, fed beast so carefully.

Never again to Egypt; Assyria shall rule him now, the unrepentant; already the sword is let loose in those towns of his, the brave shall engulf, the wise shall devour. Can my people be reconciled with me? All hangs in doubt, until at last I put a yoke on all alike, never to be taken away from them. What, Ephraim, must I abandon thee? Must I keep Israel under watch and ward? Can I let thee go the way of Adama, share the doom of Seboim? All at once my heart misgives me, and from its embers pity revives.

Read also Isaias (63.15–16):
Bethink thee now, in heaven; look down from the

palace where thou dwellest, holy and glorious. Where, now, is thy jealous love, where thy warrior's strength? Where is thy yearning of heart, thy compassion? For me, compassion is none.

Yet, who is our father, Lord, if not thou?

"Compassion": how remarkably well this word applies to God! And it is a revealed word, we must not forget. Thus, already at the time of the Old law, God was not insensible; God had compassion for his people, the heart of a Father. How can we help but think of the parable of the prodigal son, where the father as soon as he sees his son in the distance returning to him is "moved with compassion." It is in this manner that God wanted to reveal himself!*

Say: Our Father

But when our Lord appears, all voices, however great they may be, keep silent. Our Lord will speak to us of his Father with an accent of his own, with divine authority and simplicity: "God speaks well of God."

Here, let us listen to the sweet and sacred name by which he wants us to call him. "This then is to be your prayer: Our Father," or "Our Father who art in Heaven,"

* These bonds of God the Father with his people in the Old Testament should be developed at length. Cf. the stirring book of Rev. Louis Bouyer, *The Meaning of Sacred Scripture* (Notre Dame, Ind.: U. of Notre Dame Press, 1958), Chap. 11.

or "Our heavenly Father." Let us not pass over these extraordinary words. Let them come to rest in the deepest part of us, to rise again to our lips at the time of prayer.

"Father" here signifies, in its most general sense, a personal source, an enduring solicitude to which we are joined. Man is not a foundling in a universe without a soul. Man has a Father in heaven. And this bond which unites us to him is the most intimate that can be conceived: that by which we are created at every instant and engendered unto our inmost being. Everyone of us has a filial bond. And we know well that a father does not forget his children. In secrecy, to ourselves, we can murmur "Father," or "My Father," or even better "Our Father." And he hears us, for we never leave his hands. Such is the greatest secret, expressed in the most simple manner, that our Lord came to teach us. In whatever circumstances he may be, to whatever milieu he belongs, each man has a Father in heaven.

Our Lord has us call him "in heaven" or "heavenly" to indicate where his dwelling is. There is heaven and there is the world. Heaven is where God reigns, where he is fully God beyond question. And that is why there is peace in heaven. The earth is also the dwelling of God, but it is also the dwelling of man. And that is why we find struggle in it, things which pass and vanish away. However, if the will of God is done on earth as it is in heaven, then all can be at peace. Our Lord teaches us to lift our eyes above the earth: up to heaven where God is, not in order to flee the earth, but to bring, as best we can, earth and heaven into harmony; also that we may understand that the earth, however beautiful, is not heaven, and that our Father himself is in heaven. Every religious man bends his knee before the Father who is in heaven in his sacred Majesty. But his heart throbs with joy. The heavens are not empty. There is a Father waiting for him and calling him.

This Father is holy. We do not invoke him in order to feel reassured in our mediocrity, but rather that we may never be at rest in it: "You are to be perfect, as your heavenly Father is perfect" (Matt. 5.48). The Christian religious life is conceivable only as an unremitting ascent, a more and more permeating effort to be in accord with this Holy Father with a more and more total consent. Here is the only source of all truth and of all happiness.

Our Lord, then, wishes to draw us into a state of absolute sincerity with ourselves, or, better, of total transparency before God. What counts is not what men think of us (this opinion of men to which we are so sensitive), but what God thinks of us. Man must let his heavenly Father see into the very depths of his being.

Nothing is more important than this effort of the disciple of Jesus to enter into himself, and let himself be judged— without worry and without complacency—by him who sounds the loins and the hearts. Rare are the men who wear no mask, use no disguise, no excuse, but who are simple and forthright before God. That is what our Lord wants to lead us to: to live beneath the gaze of the Father, who sees what is done in secret. How *true* everything becomes then!

Thus, little by little, man becomes illumined. Let us not be mistaken: We remain of the earth and therefore we remain obscure. But he who faithfully lives in the sight of God is enlightened little by little. He comes closer to his Father: "Your light must shine so brightly before men that they can see your good works, and glorify your Father who is in heaven" (Matt. 5.16). The Father is glorified only by his children of light. Then men recognize him. When we watch closely the life of certain friends of God, our heart rejoices: God exists at last, we have found God in his children. Such is our deep vocation: We are called to make God known through our works of light: "Take good care, then, that this principle of light which is in thee is light, not darkness" (Luke 41.35).

This holy Father is also the God who forgives. He has no indulgence for evil; but he is holy to the point of burning sin away and converting the sinner. Always, our Lord has revealed his Father to us as the Father of the prodigal son. This is not subjectivism; it is pure revelation, and we must receive it with all our faith, with a soul adoring and overwhelmed. The only true God, he who reigns in heaven and on earth, is also he who is waiting for the prodigal son, and who, when he sees him from afar, takes "pity on him"

(Luke 15.20). Such is God for us. This is how our Lord spoke to us about his Father.

Therefore we can be like our Father only if we practice mercy ourselves: "Be merciful, then, as your Father is merciful" (Luke 6.36). In this light we understand better how the spirit of our Lord is the opposite of all pharisaism. How could he who has learned to live without disguise, in the sight of God, be hard and contemptuous of his brothers? He knows too well his own heart. How could he who knows that God forgave him refuse to forgive his brothers? And yet everyday we must start all over again. We see more easily the speck of dust in our brother's eye than the beam in our own. And we catch ourselves in the process of judging, twenty times a day, when our Lord simply says: "Do not judge." And if the measure we use for our brothers will be used for ourselves, how mediocre, superficial, and insignificant shall we be found who so easily find others superficial, mediocre, insignificant? Man is not merciful by nature. The Father in heaven must teach us to be merciful in the depths of ourselves: "that so you may be true sons of your Father in heaven, who makes his sun rise on the evil and equally on the good, his rain fall on the just and equally on the unjust" (Matt. 5.45). Yes, however great the hardness of life and men, we shall be disciples of Christ only if we have compassion, "bowels of mercy," for our brothers.

*He takes every hair of your head
into his reckoning*

The holy and merciful Father takes care of his children
and helps them even in their material needs. Indeed, we
must not make a romantic and false idyll out of the
providence of God. If man neither plows nor sows, God
does not give growth. If the disciple of Christ does not
suffer persecution for the sake of justice, the poor will
remain oppressed. In an even deeper manner, the providence of God does not clear up for us the obscurities of
the world. We find tragedy in the Gospel itself: a death
on the Cross. In our lives also there may be many tragic
and incomprehensible things. And yet, we must open ourselves, once and for all, to these extraordinary phrases in
which our Lord declares, in the most categorical way,
that the Father in heaven takes care of us down to the
smallest detail. Read again slowly the sixth chapter of
St. Matthew. Listen to the accent and the authority of
Christ. And you will hear the revelation of the true God,
by whom even the hairs on our head are taken into
reckoning (Luke 12.7).

At a time when in spite of ourselves we unconsciously
accept a mechanical vision of the world, when we find it
so difficult to really believe in a Personal God, how good
and how necessary it is for us to believe in this revealed
God, who watches over every detail of our life. Then only

we begin to be disciples of Jesus and to participate in his filial spirit.

We ourselves may one day be in difficult circumstances —perhaps we are already—and we shall be able to do nothing but cry out with him: "My God, my God, why has thou forsaken me?" And there will be no answer. Yet there will be his example and his last word, his supreme teaching: "Father, into thy hands I commend my spirit."

My Father and your Father

But why can we call God, whom nobody has seen, "Our Father," if not because he has adopted us in Christ? We are touching here on the central truth of the Christian Mystery. Although we cannot develop it here at any length, we know that the human race is called to an extraordinary and properly divine destiny.

Slowly, through centuries and centuries of progress and retreat, of murder and holiness, humanity has been on its way toward the "manifestation of the sons of God" (Rom. 8.19). The world does not move toward this "manifestation" on strength alone. The "sons of God" are much more than supermen, Prometheans brought slowly to the culmination of millions of years of evolution. The sons of God are the sons of grace, the sons of the infinitely holy, free and transcendent love of a Father who is in heaven and who has adopted us in his Son.

With most men the seed is weak. Yet they are truly sown as sons of God. The whole kingdom of God is enclosed in a grain, the smallest of seeds. This seed is placed in the depths of our being. But one day our real selves shall be manifested in what we are, and then we shall be like God because we shall see him as he is. But right now, with Jesus and in him, we can call him "Father, . . . our Father who art in heaven."

11 Lord, Teach Us How to Pray
(Luke 11.1)

Our Lord not only reveals his Father to us; he also teaches us to speak to him. And to speak to God as to a Father is to pray. This mysterious intercourse between man and God, heart to heart with him, is implied in every page of the Gospel. Here we would like to outline the real essence of prayer.

It has often been said that the major, decisive word of our Lord on prayer is the one he places on our lips when he teaches us to pray: "When you pray, say: Our Father. . . ." This is the principal revelation to which we must always come back. Christian prayer is the response of the soul adopted by God. To pray we must know that we are adopted, that we are addressing ourselves to a listening God, and we must know it from within.

We know this in a twofold way: on the one hand, through the objective revelation of our Lord "preserved" by his Church: Christ's own word, "You will say: Our Father." We know it, on the other hand, through the personal, incommunicable revelation of his Holy Spirit to each living soul in the Church. And this is no illusion either.

We have a text of St. Paul in which this mysterious, yet certain, revelation of the Holy Spirit is taught to us:

> The spirit you have now received is not, as of old, a spirit of slavery, to govern you by fear; it is the spirit of adoption, which makes us cry out, Abba, Father. The Spirit himself thus assures our spirit, that we are children of God. And the Spirit comes to the aid of our weakness; when we do not know what prayer to offer, to pray as we ought, the Spirit intercedes for us, with groans beyond all utterance. (Rom. 8.15–26).

This text is absolutely essential to understanding the essence of prayer. The soul of prayer is the Holy Spirit himself, who assures our spirit that we are adopted and thus has us shout: Abba, Father.* Christian prayer, in its foundation, is a mystery. It is the first awakening of the adopted soul stammering the proper name of God: Abba, Father, or, Christ, my Lord and my God.

In this light, we can say that Christian prayer is like the language of God, which he teaches us patiently during the course of our life. Indeed, when we pray, it is we who are speaking. But who has formed this word on our lips and,

---

* By this we do not mean to say that Christian prayer is addressed to God the Father only, but that it is also addressed to the God of Grace, the living and revealed God, Father, Son, and Spirit, who calls us by having us born from him.

even more, in our heart? It is God who teaches us his language. In a like manner the newborn child cannot speak. It is his mother who awakens him to the words by speaking to him first. She calls him and her call forms the word in him, the word which is his answer. And he answers in the language of his mother tongue. The same applies to the newborn of grace, re-born of the Holy Spirit of God. God has informed us, God has spoken first, and through the action of his word which the soul was finally able to hear, it understood that it was adopted, that God was living and listening to it, and it spoke in its turn. But this word which is prayer, was the very language of God which the soul was stammering when it pronounced the Sacred Name, Abba, Father. Thus, God teaches us his tongue in the course of our life through the prayer he arouses in our hearts. Then we understand better the call of his disciples: "Lord, teach us how to pray"; for, of ourselves, we do not know how to pray, how to speak. But if our soul is spoken to, it will respond, like the child awakening to his mother's life. This means that in order to learn how to pray, we must first bewail the fact that we do not know how to pray; we must turn toward him who is the only one who can teach us from within: "Teach us how to pray." A new language must take shape in us.

The language of prayer is formed in the depths of our heart, for here is its privileged place. Indeed we pray with our whole being, our lips, our body even (the sacred gestures of Liturgy); but the birthplace of prayer, if we may say so, is in the depths of our heart. We know what the Holy Scripture means by "heart." Not the sensitive or the affective nature which is the most exterior in us, not the intellectual alone, but the root of our thoughts and our love, the most intimate, the truest, depth, where our great thoughts and our great decisions are made, where we are alone with our Creator: "Pray to your Father in secret." It is this heart that speaks to God in prayer. For it has a language that God understands—more deeply than that which comes from the lips of man. He understands what comes from man's heart: blessing or curse, joy or bitterness, faith or doubt, confidence or distrust, love or selfishness. *Deus cui omne cor patet et omnis voluntas loquitur* ("God for whom all hearts are open and every will is speaking"), the Church has us say in a prayer to the Holy Spirit, before the celebration of Mass.

And our deepest heart is that which was formed by our deepest, ultimate love. We know the importance Christian doctrine gives to this utmost love in which man finds his rest. Most of the time, this love is disentangled with great difficulty, since it is exposed to many rivalries. Yet it always exists, and our heart speaks according to it. Such speech is prayer; it is the language of our deepest love. And this is important, for if we pray little it is probably because we have little love. We have not set our heart on God, on Christ. And yet we love them more deeply than we realize.

They never cease to create anew this heart made for them. We are directly related to them; we already live face to face with them in faith. Therefore, it is very important that we should know how to retire into the depth of our heart to hear it speak. If prayer was but the language of our brain, we could pray by laboriously conceiving ideas about God; if prayer was but the movement of our lips, we could speak to God and speak to men at the same time. But prayer is first of all in the depth of our heart, and can, by right, always exist, even when our fingers are busy or when our lips speak to men, or when our troubled mind is full of worries. The language of prayer is born in an even greater depth: in the depth of the heart that loves God. In final analysis, it is our love that speaks and prays.

It is supremely important that we always try to pray in our heart, for God listens to this heart and teaches it the language of love.

What are the themes of this language? They are as varied as each soul. Yet, they can be reduced to three principal themes that may be said to constitute the "music of the soul."

There is the theme of childlike adoration and love. In it the soul simply stammers the divine name: "God; Our God; Our Father; O great God; Holy God; Great God of Love; Christ; Our Christ; Holy Spirit of Love." Each soul has its language and its rhythm.

Then there is the theme of blessing, a natural part of the

fundamental harmony of the Christian soul. God listens to
what comes from our heart: blessing or curse. How the
heart that blesses him even in worries and trials of life
glorifies him!

There is the theme of petition, a very fundamental one,
for are we not always poor and expecting? And what are
we expecting? Daily bread, the forgiveness of our sins,
the strength to bear the weight of trials, the coming of the
Kingdom of God, and, above all, the holy will of God
present on earth as it is in heaven. And expectations can
glorify God if they are in accordance with the spirit of
prayer that his Son taught us.

Now, what are the difficulties of this divine language?

There is God's silence and our little faith. For God often
keeps silent and tries our faith. We have prayed to him
so many times and have heard no answer. Here we must
learn not to base our prayer upon sentiment or upon its
fulfillment, but upon the sole word of our Lord in which
we have faith. Prayer, in order to be born in our heart,
requires an act of faith in the word of Christ: "Ask, and
you shall receive; seek, and you shall find; knock, and the
door shall be opened to you."

There is also our lack of silence. We said that there
were two parts in us: the acting part and the listening part.
Both are necessary and good when they are informed by
charity. But the best, the deepest, is the part that listens.

When the soul no longer listens, it no longer prays. We must defend this interior silence at all cost. It is a good rule to try to keep always in us a spirit of silence, no matter what we are doing. Otherwise action engulfs us and our heart can no longer pray.

There are, finally, the limitations of our nature. Physical fatigue, nervous strain, all kinds of depressions undermine our prayer. Here again we must strive to keep our balance. There are moods above which we should rise, which we have no right to accept as an habitual state. However, when we are overcome, there remains the obligation to pray with our weakness. If we offer it to God, it becomes prayer. God does not despise a contrite and humbled heart. We may only have our poverty to offer, but the prayer of the poor is dear to him. We may have nothing more than sadness, but such was our Lord's Agony and his prayer in the Garden.

Thus everything can become prayer and the soul can tend to pray always.

12 Everyone That Asks, Will Receive
(Luke 11.9)

Prayer of petition

The prayer of which the Gospel speaks most explicitly is the prayer of petition. Here our Lord appears singularly more human than those magnificent masters who consider contemplation the only prayer worthy of God. True contemplatives know well that they are always beggars. The humble prayer of petition implies the most sublime contemplation. Does it not depend fundamentally on the complete gratuitousness of God? Our Lord thus wants to teach us that our fundamental condition is that of real indigence entrusting itself to him. To live with Christ in one's heart is to throw oneself with joy, at every instant, upon the Saviour who holds all riches. An authentic Christian prayer of petition is to be found at the bottom of the heart of every true disciple of Jesus. The latter lives depending on grace as a child depends upon its father. Our filial dependence with respect to this prayer is a law of our life that will never end. Here we find the secret of great strength and great meekness.

Our Lord insistently recommends this humble and trusting prayer of petition at the time of temptation. Few of his words are as earnest as those he said in the Garden of Olives: "The spirit is willing but the flesh is weak. Watch and pray." We must watch, for the Evil One is close by, and the flesh is weak. The resilience of Christian strength lies in a piety filled with love and faith in God who loves us. Temptation can be blessed because it shows us our weakness. We can no longer doubt. We shall no longer count ourselves with the just for whom Christ did not come, but with the sinners he came to save. We know from experience that we must call upon God for help, and that we must not leave him for one single instant. Now from the depths of our soul comes humble and ardent prayer: "Have mercy, Lord, for I am a sinner . . . and yet I believe that I love you and trust you who have come for sinners." And if we fall, our call to the purity of Christ will be more vehement: "May you be blessed, O God, who wanted to be a God of forgiveness."

We shall also humbly realize our fragility with respect to our temporal needs. God wants us to talk to him about them. Health, food, clothing, rent—all this is included in the daily bread that our Lord teaches us to ask for. Indeed our desires must be formulated in a certain order. "Make it your first care to find the kingdom of God, and his approval, and all things shall be yours without the asking." Our Lord does not want us to be anxious, but filled with all intrepid joy and abandoned in the hands of his Father.

Yet, he knows the human condition. He knows that there are men who are starving and who have no shelter. He expects courage, but he is waiting for our prayer. He wants us to stand fast without giving up. All these worries of ours—they must become prayer. They must be turned into faith and confidence; we must present them to God again and again. We must not distrust him, not even for one instant. Listen to his words: "Man of little faith, why did you doubt?" "Everything is possible to him who believes." "O woman, how great is your faith. Be it done as you wish."

With this kind of intrepid prayer the saints accomplished astonishing things. They laid their indigence before God: need for money, ill health, children to be fed. They did not doubt. They acted. And God heard their prayer. "And I say to you: Ask, and you shall receive; seek, and you shall find; knock, and the door shall be opened to you." Word of God, full of meaning, bewildering to our faith! The Lord continues to teach us to pray in this manner: Let your worries not overwhelm you, let them not disturb your soul. Cast them upon God, your silence will be your strength. Walk on confidently. Am I not with you?

And in times of human distress, Mary the Mother of Jesus, is also with us.

"Your will be done. . . ." This is the last word of the prayer of petition. Through it, our desires are well-ordered and the soul can have peace, true peace, that derives from the accepted truth. Let us understand it well. Indeed, we are speaking already of resignation, and this word, though often discredited, is Christian. For the soul does not resign itself to fatalism. Even as it is broken, it abandons itself to hands that it knows to be wise. But this cry, "Your will be done," can also express an ardent and vehement desire. "Yes, I wish it ardently; I ask you, Lord, that your will be done in me and in the world." We cannot ask for anything greater. This prayer of petition is already an act of love and the most perfect of all; that which harmonizes our will with the will of God and Christ. This act of love can be an habitual state of prayer. The will of the saints was never at variance with the will of God. It was their deepest hunger, their truest desire. Jesus said: "My meat is to do the will of him who sent me." This is the meat for strong souls, nourishment beyond sentiment, supporting us in times of desolation. Little Sister Theresa said before she died: "What reassures me is that I have never done my will." And above all there is the word of our Lord in the Garden of Olives: "Only as thy will is, not as mine is. . . ."

Indeed, the profession that gives a sense of fulfillment or else the simple means of earning a living, the duties we love and those that devour us, the agreeable task and the crucifying labor, everything must become prayer in us. Take everything that happens to you: the annoying brother, the work to be started once again, the task that means death to your self, and make it your meat, murmur-

ing with great love: "Only as your will is, not as mine is."
And the Lord will say those blessed words to you: "If
anyone does the will of my Father who is in heaven, he
is my brother, and my sister, and my mother."

We must pray continually

Then everything can become prayer. But we have come
upon the principle of this divine alchemy: We must live
with God, with Christ, in us.

Indeed, it is necessary to set a time for silence and prayer
to accomplish anything serious. However, our resolutions
will be but a flash in the sky if we do not have the will to
live habitually with Christ as with a friend. We must begin
a conversation, we must look for a Presence. Ultimately,
we must love a Person, the infinite Person of the Word-
made-flesh, Jesus of Nazareth, Saviour of our misery and
life of our life, unique Master to whom we turn: "Lord,
teach us how to pray."

13 Give Thanks Continually to God
(Eph. 5.18)

Our Lord taught us to speak with God as with our Father, and this is prayer. He taught us to express our needs to him, our desires, and this is the prayer of petition. But we must also, and at the same time, give thanks to him and praise him. He wants to see in us souls who like to thank and who, far from falling back upon themselves, thank with full hearts. Let our souls expand in his praise.

Bless and damn not

There is a harmful tendency in us, negative, destructive, pessimistic, which leads us to see evil everywhere and to emphasize it. We then take the attitude of accusers. We accuse everything, our brothers, events, things, except, maybe, ourselves. Without realizing it, we accuse God himself. We practically judge his work to be bad. Sometimes even, we accuse him directly and consciously. Revolt against him and blasphemy suddenly surge from our heart to our lips. Who knows his own heart? Sometimes, even often, it is against ourselves that this evil pleasure to destroy turns itself. We accuse ourselves, alas! not with the humble peace of the sinner before his Saviour, but with disappointment or rage, or simply with a bitter weariness. We have deceived ourselves to such a great extent.

All this is not the work of God, but of the Evil One. It is not without reason that the Scripture calls him the Accuser, he who ceaselessly accuses. What is he accusing? Everything—men, events, things, in one word, God's work. Because he has excluded himself from it, he tries to destroy it, insinuating that it is badly made. We must realize this: Every time we give in to this negative, accusing inclination, it is to evil that we give in. It is that spirit that speaks in us, not the Spirit of God.

The inspiration coming from God is altogether different. It induces us to bless and praise. For to praise is to proclaim that he is rightly said "to be God," justly called God. Then the soul is liberated. It does not remain under evil's unconscious influence, but it shouts for joy and proclaims that everything he did, God did well. It is Mary's song in her *Magnificat*, Zacharias' in the *Benedictus*, the aged Simeon's in the *Nunc dimittis*; it is the song which was heard at the birth of the Saviour: "Glory to God in the highest, and peace on earth to men of good will." The soul who can praise is a liberated soul. In it everything is reconciled. It is just, it does not grumble any longer. It is a "Yes" to God, an Amen. It is in his love. It does not come out of it. It is in harmony with him.

Confess to God that he is good

First of all, it is to God that it addresses itself, happy to exclaim: "Blessed be you, my God." It says it shouting for joy, or sweetly whispers it. Yes, blessed be he, for he is God. There is, no doubt, much evil disfiguring his work, but he remains good. In him, there is no evil.

This deep prayer of praise is the foundation of all Christian prayer and also of the prayer of petition. In his most disinterested contemplation, the saint does not forget that he is essential mendicity and he prays forever with his hands open to receive. In the same way, he proclaims with his whole being that God is good. We cannot pray without confessing, at least implicitly, that God is God and that he is good. This deep and happy gratitude, even when not formulated, is the prayer of praise.

It is the accent of the prayer of the Church, psalms, hymns, *Gloria in Excelsis, Te Deum.* All proclaim with joy that God is God, and that it is he who created us, and not ourselves. Only he is God, only he is holy, only he is the Lord. Our prayer should be penetrated, little by little, with this spirit and become like the breathing of the soul, being in turn joyful and meek, exulting or secret. . . . "Yes, blessed be you, my God. And I am happy to confess that only you are God and only you are good."

Thus, our spiritual attitude would be more true and

open. Without ever abandoning the humble and confident prayer of petition, we would be filled with God rather than with ourselves. God's glory, his goodness, his beauty, man's acknowledgment of him, would mean more to us. That is the meaning of the liturgical prayer: "Let your contentment be in the Holy Spirit, your tongues unloosened in psalms and hymns and spiritual music, as you sing and give praise to the Lord in your hearts. Give thanks continually to God our Father, in the name of our Lord Jesus Christ" (Eph. 5.18–19). Few texts are as rich; very few give us such an understanding of the true religion of Christ.

That all that is joy in me may bless the Lord

We must, then, learn to discover our joys and let them praise God. They are numerous. We all have some. We need but be attentive to them. Let us not be overwhelmed with worries and the sadness of the world. Let us open our eyes and bless: a friendly hand, a kind word, a letter, a comforting, the smile of a child, sunshine, a flower. Dare we say that we have no joys!

It is up to us to transform them into prayer. Indeed, there is in us a terrible flightiness that leads us, as soon as we are satisfied, to forget God and rush toward our happiness without thinking of him. Moreover, we are all inclined to a spiritual stinginess which makes us cling to joy with gluttony. And yet, of itself, joy is a daughter of God, even more directly than suffering. It is an authentic way to him. It takes but a poor and pure heart to refer its joy back to God and therewith to find it anew, marvellously purified. It has now become prayer.

Then our joys will truly praise God and freely fly to him, or sweetly whisper in us. Far from binding our hearts to the world, our joys will direct them toward God. St. Dominic falls spontaneously on his knees to receive bread given to him. Is it not God who nourishes his poor people?

To give thanks, thus appears to be the virtue of the poor. The rich give no thanks. The man who is truly poor in spirit, according to Christ, never ceases to thank God for everything. He knows very well in his inner being that nothing is due to him. For him, everything is grace. How good God is to him! And, in fact, God *is* good to him. God loves to enter the life of the poor with his infinite liberality.

Look at your own life. Become aware of your joys; they are more numerous than you think. Be not ungrateful, but with a deep and thankful heart, and not a light or avaricious one, learn to transform your joys into prayer by directing them to God. And, even above your joys, there is the joy of the Lord and of his Mother, and that of his friends, the saints. They all exist to uplift your heart!

Winter and frost, bless the Lord

There are not only joys. There are also "winter and frost." This psalm of the *Benedicite* that we use for thanksgiving after communion is rather curious. Everything is intermingled in a fraternal blessing: sun and moon, quadrupeds and birds, whales and large fishes, children of men and the just. Not everything in it, however, is agreeable. There are wind and rain, frost and winter. And yet we have them all bless God joyfully.

What are the frost and winter if not all the daily annoyances and trials of life? And when they are beating into our face, the psalm invites us to transform them into the blessing and praise of God.

First there are the annoyances, irritations, inconveniences, and unexpected vexations that assail us every day. Why not thank God for them? Why not make the best of it joyfully, once and for all, and if once is not sufficient, let us do so anew at the beginning of every day. However, it is not so easy, for to change into blessing everything that irritates and exasperates us, implies an astonishing surrender of one's self to others in love. If you do try though, you will find amazing strength in it, the source of great joy, and a great peace of soul. But you must love God enough to rejoice about your annoyances, not, of course, because they irritate you, but because they provide you with a great opportunity to offer yourself to God with joy and truth: "Frost and winter, bless the Lord. . . ."

The very thing that upsets me, I offer to you, Lord, and even with joy, for it can generate love in my poor heart. Troublesome telephone calls, squalling children, bless the Lord. . . .

There are finally the great sufferings and trials. Here, we must let God take over. Only he is powerful enough to transform them slowly into thanksgiving. But how pleasing to God is a spark of love and submission from a broken heart. A heart that could have damned, but is now blessing. What caused this miracle if not love?

Jesus, let my joy remain

This is what is so marvelous: So many things could destroy joy. How many hearts have ceased to bless? In how many lives is there still a gushing spring of blessings and not a bitter stream of rancour and resentment? When God listens to our hearts, does he still hear the sweet accents of thanksgiving, or are they filled with discontent and bitterness? We understand now this cry of the soul that Bach expresses in a choral: "Jesus, let my joy remain"; not for myself, but for you; to protest that you are God, that you are good, that you do not deceive me. O God, you were the delight of my soul, do not cease to be the delight of my old age. When a soul can praise God in

this manner, after journeying through life, how great it is
and how it glorifies God. As for us, we pray with fervent
love: "Jesus, let my joy remain."

Every day, almost every minute, the holy Host, the pure
Host, the immaculate Host, the Eucharist of the Lord, the
eternal and substantial Thanksgiving, is elevated from the
earth. With it, in it, let us exclaim to God from the depths
of our heart that he is good, that he has done all things well,
yes all things, even this evil that he has permitted and that
the love of his Son can slowly change into love.

*Let us give thanks to God always and for all things,
through our Lord Jesus Christ, to God our Father.*

14 Pray to Thy Father in Secret
(Math. 6.6)

Christian prayer consists basically of an essential petition
and an essential thanksgiving. Taught by his Master, the
disciple of Christ must learn to live constantly depending
on grace and continually giving thanks. But this blessed
state of supplication and of thanksgiving tends also to become a humble, but tenacious, desire for intimacy with
God. Is it not there that God wants to lead us? "But when
you are praying, go into your inner room and shut the door
upon yourself, and so pray to thy Father in secret."

Intimacy with God

Are we allowed to use the very word "intimacy" when
we speak of God? How can we sinners, clinging to the
obscure realities of the earth, dream of an intimacy with
God? And supposing that some rare, privileged souls may
use this term, how could the majority of men, involved in
the fight for existence, pretend to it?

And yet, we must emphasize it: Our Lord came to teach
us that the will of his Father is to entertain in each of us

personal relations of faith and love. The alliance he wants to conclude with men, his kingdom that he wants to establish in them, is in their heart. What does that mean if not a desire for intimacy? Let us not be afraid to say so and to repeat it: Everything in Christianity is oriented toward this personal communication of God with his children. If it does not exist at least as a desire, we find ourselves still in the position of the Jews, under the yoke of the law and not in the liberty of the Holy Spirit and of love. God is as yet but a law, or a more or less demanding and troublesome moral postulate to us. He is not yet the personal God our Lord came to reveal to us. He has not yet made his abode in our heart.

And why? We must come to the great statement of St. John which seems to be the last word of Christian revelation: "God is love." And let us banish from this statement any complex of squeamish sensitivity that horrifies many and rightly so. Let us take it in the extraordinary sense of the revelation. "God so loved the world, that he gave up his only begotten Son. . . . At this we recognized love, that he gave his life for us. . . . And we believed." That is what we earnestly profess to believe, when we call ourselves Christians.

Thus, if a God of Love has visited his people through the Incarnation, has redeemed them through the Cross, nourished them through the Eucharist, and made his abode in us, why should we not find him where he is? And that is everywhere: in our churches, in our tabernacles, and in the depths of ourselves as well as of our brothers, whether we are joyful or sorrowful, in the liberty of our soul or in its bondage. Why should we not learn patiently to talk to him or keep silent in front of him? To love him as he loves us, to suffer with him, and to draw from him at every moment this marvellous and divine love our brothers demand from us? This is not any kind of illuminism or the privilege of souls that are retired from the world; it is the strong and substantial revelation of Christ offered to all who believe in him. For, after all, that is what is difficult: to dare believe in him up to this point; to go as far as to think that beyond the unfolding of our sins, social injustices, the evil of men, our trials and solitudes, there is a God of Love waiting for us to converse with him in secret. "But when you are praying, pray to thy Father in secret."

The part in us that listens

But in order to learn to converse with God, there must be silence in us, and what we might call "the part in us that listens" must have been developed.

The Gospel tells us the story of Mary who took her place at the Lord's feet, and listened to his words. It was her manner of showing her love. Her sister Martha showed hers by waiting on the many needs of serving. And if Martha's serving was agreeable to the Lord, we are told that Mary's silence was even more pleasing to him. "Mary has chosen for herself the best part of all." What does this mean? She has chosen the part that listens to the Word of Christ.

Each of us has this mysterious part in himself. Let us not be afraid to say it is the most valuable part. Already on the plane of human realities, it is an easily established truth: man confides only what he has already listened to inside himself. This is true of the artist, it is true of the humble of heart who knows how to love, it is true of whoever has something to give. But it is even more true and infinitely mysterious when we speak of God. God speaks to man. There is in us a part made to listen to him. We cannot locate this part, nor do we know what language it understands. We only know that there is such a part and that it is listening to God when it has suddenly become silent and mysterious. Our Lord speaks of it as a reality, a mysterious one indeed, but as real, and more so, than the exterior voice striking the human ear. Blessed is he who through grace can live on this plane: "Blessed is he who hears God's Word." We must believe in this part in us and not allow it to die, buried under the weight of worldly worries.

Close the door and open your heart

But to this end we must be able to keep silent, and as the Gospel teaches us, we must "close the door upon ourselves." Close it to all empty sounds: exaggerated worries, resentment, hurt pride, anxiety which dissipates and exhausts us.

Let us not misunderstand, however. It is not, of course, a question of escaping the real conditions of existence and taking refuge in indifference to men and the events of the world. We must be present, not like a straw carried away in a whirlwind, but as a profound being who, if it pleases God, can reassure his brothers because his heart is calm. That is to say, we must fight at any price to keep our silence. The more worried we are, the harder the battle is, the more we must keep silent. It is a question of spiritual life or death. We do not hesitate to say that a being who has no silence in itself cannot remake itself. It is doomed to dispersion and to sterility. "It is in your hope and your silence that you will find your strength," says the Scripture. We must be able, then, to shut the door of our soul to the vain sounds that call to us; it is a task of every instant. But there are privileged hours. The example of our Lord gives us the hours. It was during the night, or in the early morning, that he used to go up to the mountain or to a deserted place; and there he prayed. It is generally during the quiet of the night that the soul is most silent, when the sounds of the day are dying down or when they have not yet started. It may be up to our own ability to take advantage of it, each according to his special vocation: one in the early morning, another during his sleeplessness, a third on a solitary walk on his way home from work. Let us find out. No doubt, we will find a moment when the soul is habitually more silent. Let us consider this moment sacred. It is God's time.

This is how we can open our hearts. Christian silence is not emptiness. It is the consciousness of the more profound soul who, on this level, finds again its brothers. For if we do keep silent, it is in order to open ourselves to God and to his Love. All Christian sanctity is ultimately founded upon communicating with the love of God in Jesus Christ. Now, this love has loved men even to the Cross. It was patient, strong, magnanimous. To open ourselves to him is to open ourselves to our brothers. It means to look at the Cross and to love it because in this way we resemble him. Silence teaches us that all this, because it is, after all, a Person whom we find again in a mysterious way: the Father who is in heaven or his incarnate Son.

Keep the word of God

Here we must turn to the master of prayer and ask him to deepen our soul, so that we may not forget, but are able to "keep" his word. We find this word "keep" several times in the Gospel: "Blessed is he who hears the word of God and keeps it"; and "Mary kept all these things in her heart." Here we find the secret of intimate prayer. It implies that the soul is profound and is not at the mercy of the winds.

It keeps what God has entrusted to it: a certain light, a phrase of his Gospel, a prayer of his Church, a word of his priest, a visit in holy communion, a certain trial, a cross to bear. All this can be the word of God and germinate in the soul, but the deep memory of the soul must keep it. Then the Word of the Gospel grows in the soul and bears fruit in it, and this fruit is called meekness, peace, joy, gentleness, strength, courage.

Let us learn to open our soul to God and to keep his Word. And through the worries of life as well as through the even more terrible spiritual discouragements, and in spite of the apparent silence of God testing his friends, let us not abandon this tenacious and ardent search for intimacy with God. And God will finally yield. "And the grain that fell in good soil stands for those who hear the word, and hold it with a noble and generous heart, and endure, and yield a harvest" (Luke 8.15).

15 And He Passed the Whole Night Offering Prayer to God

(Luke 6.12)

To pray is to speak to God in one's heart. On this level, prayer is a way of life and an unceasing process. However, there are rhythms, and privileged times. The Gospel teaches us, here again, a valuable lesson: Even the Lord submitted himself to rhythms in his prayer.

It is essential to the rhythm of prayer that it tend to become unceasing. As always the Lord gives us the example: "I am not alone because the Father is with me" (John 16. 32). He never ceased to speak to him. And neither are we ever alone: God, Christ, are always with us. Why should our heart cease to be attracted to them? Seen in this light, there is no impenetrable wall between prayer and life. To pray is to live, to live fully, but it is, so to speak, to live with another. Joy or sadness, work or rest, worries or peace, we must learn to share all things with Christ and never act as if we were living alone. Here as always, love is the principle of this "life with another." He who truly loves God and Christ, tends to do everything with them; his heart tends to speak with them unceasingly. We have indeed our overwhelming occupations, and the hard struggle for life does not spare us. But, here again, we are never alone. Why should we resign ourselves to live as if we were alone? Even the businessman, tormented by worries, must, if he is a Christian, try to cast his cares upon God at every moment. God is with him in his struggles. He never completely loses sight of God, and so the prayer of his heart never ceases.

It is supremely important that we train ourselves to live always with God in our heart and to speak to him often. No doubt, a specific time consecrated to prayer is necessary, but it is even more necessary that we have an abiding awareness of God. What are we waiting for to join God? A sudden flash in the depth of our soul? Until our work is finished? Here we are mistaken. We must never put off turning to God in our heart. We must do it at the very moment he comes to our mind. Eternal life really begins here. "Why do you delay, my soul, since you can love God in your heart, henceforth?" (St. John of the Cross).

If prayer must tend to be permanent, there are, however, privileged times for it. Here again, let us take note of the teachings of the Lord.

Although Christ prayed always, he still preferred to pray alone at night or in the early morning. The Gospel says it expressly, and few things are as moving as these brief and precise notes evoking the holy humanity of Christ. "Then, at early dawn, he left them, and went away to a lonely place, and began praying there" (Mark 1.35). "It was at this time that he went out on to the mountain side, and passed the whole night offering prayer to God" (Luke 6.12).

Thus our Lord teaches us, through his example, that we should pray preferably at night when the spirit is no more or not yet distracted by noises of the day. In one sense, nocturnal prayer is eternal in the Church. It is natural to the religious soul. It is very moving to think that in his holy humanity the Lord chose to follow the laws of our nature.

In practice, we know what great questions this "rhythm of the night" raises. And we know how varied vocations are, as varied as the temperaments and the ways of living. However, it seems that if the sacred character of the night disappeared, a definite weakening of prayer in our lives and in the Church would be felt. The tradition of the Church is unanimous with reference to this subject: The night belongs to God in a very special manner.

Still, everyone will carry out this law in a very different fashion. The Carthusian will get up during the night; the Carmelite will stay up late; the Benedictine will get up in the early morning; the mother of a family woken by her children will, in a flash, lift her heart to God; the father will soothe his worried mind by putting himself into God's hands, in the evening. But the law remains and we must make efforts to keep it: God has a right to listen to our heart, especially during the sacred time of night. The ideal is not to go to bed dead-tired, completely unable to think, or to get up already filled with the worries of the day. The truth toward which we must tend, consists in falling asleep talking to God as to a friend, and waking up lifting one's heart joyfully toward him who exists forever and whom the shadows of sleep have not dissipated.

Our Lord teaches us a second lesson through his manner of praying: Most certainly he prays everywhere, and yet he prefers a deserted place, a mountain to which he retires to pray. Again, read the Gospel. How close to us the Lord appears with the need for solitude that his holy, human soul wanted to feel. This is another valuable lesson: We must aspire to be the leaven in the dough, we must tend to pray always and everywhere, and yet it is not forbidden—the Lord even asks us—to have blessed solitudes (as long as it is not evasion) where we can find our soul again, and especially where we can meet with him, the Lord.

These solitudes will be as infinitely varied as the souls: contemplative houses, receiving monasteries, simple village church, or even more simply a place in our own home. It is important to know that there are places in which prayer is born more spontaneously in the soul, and we must not hesitate to take advantage of such places.

Our Lord, finally, teaches us a third lesson concerning his manner of praying. He sanctified the Day of the Lord and the great religious feasts of his people. Here again, the Gospel remarks expressly: "And he went into the synagogue there, as his custom was, on the sabbath day" (Luke 4.16). St. John used the great feasts of Easter, Pentecost, Dedication, Tabernacles, during which the Lord went to Jerusalem, as a chronological frame for the Lord's ministry. The conclusions to be drawn from this fact are multiple: The prayer of Christ was not simply solitary, it was mingled with the prayer of his brothers in the liturgical celebration. He prayed reciting Psalms; he submitted himself to a Church, he who will found the eternal Church and the eternal Liturgy in his blood. He celebrated the Passover of his people, he who will bequeath to us the new Passover in his Eucharist. All this has immense importance. But we would like to formulate here the essential rhythm of Christian prayer which is the rhythm of Sunday.

The attention of the faithful has often been drawn on this often forgotten Day of the Lord. Let us simply say that we must tend to make it a day of festivity and also a day of more intimate conversation with God. A day of festivity first of all for our soul, which must shake off its sadness and remember that every Sunday is Easter; for our body also that must rest, for our children who must rejoice, for our brothers whom we must receive or visit. It should also be a day of more intimate conversation with God, for, if we do find time to see our best friend on Sunday, we must not forget that our best friend, incomparably, is God, is Christ. On Sunday, our soul must, in one way or another, have the opportunity to dwell with God at length. And if this is not possible (as may often be the case), our heart must at least join God in silence and tell him of its joy and its confidence.

Rhythm of the night, rhythm of retreat, rhythm of the Day of the Lord, these are organic rhythms which our Lord himself wanted to adopt for his prayer. The servant is not greater than the master. We also must respect these rhythms.

We must now speak of the rhythms that destroy prayer, for, unfortunately, they do exist. We shall mention but two, that of feverish excitement and that of caprice. The soul that really wants to pray cannot submit habitually to these rhythms.

To the rhythm of excitement we shall oppose the calm and soothing word of the Lord to Martha: "How many cares and troubles thou hast. But only one thing is necessary" (Luke 10.41). What an answer to our restlessness: One thing is necessary. No doubt, we all have a heavy burden of work in our lives, but we also have many needless agitations, exaggerated problems, useless steps, means taken for ends. The more work we have, the closer to God we must remain.

To the rhythm of caprice, we shall oppose the thirty years of the hidden life of our Lord. He voluntarily submitted himself to the monotony of daily work. That is how the grain of wheat dies. And yet the horizons of the soul remain free. For where there is love, every day is new. For certain natures, regularity is exhausting. They must learn to find their own rhythm. But they must not consent habitually to the rhythm of caprice; prayer gets lost in it.

Let us examine our heart so as to find the deep rhythms that the Author of our nature has placed in it, and that the Lord himself adopted so humbly in his prayer.

16 Christ's Love Is a Compelling Motive

(II Cor. 5.14)

The Gospel unites in a unique and transcendent manner the sense of God and the sense of man. "None is good, except God only" (Mark 10.18). And at the same time St. John tells us: "No man has ever seen God; but if we love one another, then we have God dwelling in us" (I John 4.12). In Christianity, fraternal love has always been the sign and the effect of the love of God. This is an extremely important point. To unite constantly in the same mystery the love of Christ and the true love of our brothers, this can be the sign of Christian maturity.

Let us first ask ourselves where this fraternal love has its source. Here, our Lord has us raise our eyes. Christian fraternal love comes from a source higher than the earth. It does not consist in the simple openness of a naturally good heart; it is not simply human solidarity, as valuable and as powerful as this may be. It comes directly from God himself; from the heart of Christ for men: "Be merciful, as your Father is merciful" (Luke 6.36). And St. Paul will say: "The love of Christ [that which is in Christ] is a compelling motive" (II Cor. 5.14). Fraternal love is, to be quite accurate, the love that is in Christ for us and which moves our will, our heart, and our hands.

Henri Bergson notes expressly in his *Two Sources of Morality and Religion* that there is a difference of nature and not only of degree between human solidarity and Christian charity.* It is a love of a different nature. Human solidarity moves, so to speak, on a horizontal plane: It extends itself to those bound by a similar destiny, but by the same token it opposes itself to those bound by a different destiny. Charity moves on a vertical plane: It goes up to God and includes all men, even those whom we oppose on the horizontal plane through affinities, temperaments, milieux, conflicting interests. A natural community forms the cement of solidarity (and wounded nature terribly partitions communities). The cement of fraternal charity is the very love which encloses all men in God and in Christ. This same love transforms our heart and animates it with a new life. Therefore, it can accomplish the miracle of having us love those whom we oppose on the natural level.

This love will spontaneously express itself in two different ways, based upon the same divine reality: it will go back to the Father in heaven; it will flow from the side of Christ who loves men.

Our Lord teaches us to go back continually to the Father in heaven. Only there shall we learn a selfless and patient

* Henri Bergson, *Two Sources of Morality and Religion* (New York: Doubleday Anchor, 1954).

love, which does not look for a reward, is not discouraged by failure, and participates in the infinite generosity of the Father. And let us not conceive this recourse to the Father in heaven as a simple moral imitation which would run the risk of being inefficacious; a new birth is really needed and that is the work of God himself. We become the sons of the Most High insofar as he teaches us interiorly his way of loving:

> Why, what credit is it to you, if you love those who love you? Even sinners love those who love them. . . . No, it is your enemies you must love, and do them good, and lend to them, without any hope of return; then your reward will be a rich one, and you will be true sons of the Most High, generous like him toward the thankless and unjust. (Luke 6.32)

This is how far we must go in order to learn to love God. St. Paul tells us where he found this great fountain of charity on earth: in the Heart of Christ himself: "The love of Christ compels us." By this we understand the love that is in Christ, that comes from Christ. This love "compels" us. In the Greek original, St. Luke puts the same word on the lips of the Lord himself: "It is fire that I have come to spread over the earth, and what better wish can I have than that it should be kindled? There is a baptism I must needs be baptized with, and how impatient [I am compelled] am

I for its accomplishment" (Luke 12.49). The charity which was in Christ compelled him, gripped his heart, filled him with anguish for our salvation. It is this charity that fills us in fraternal love. Here is the living and eternal source of the missionary zeal of the Church. St. Paul was probably thinking of Christ when he wrote his great hymn to charity: "Charity is patient, is kind . . . sustains, believes, hopes, endures to the last" (I Cor. 13.4). The charity of Christ compelled him. We in turn must ask God and Christ for some of this fraternal charity, if only as much as a mustard seed.

One way of weakening fraternal charity in its substance would be to underline its supernatural nature so as to take away its real and concrete character. According to this conception, we would love men "in God" in an almost abstract manner, that is we would not love them really. It takes a long time to understand this truth, this realism of fraternal love which is practically the mark of the saints. Most of the time our fraternal charity is "idealistic." We merely love our brothers "in Christ," with sentiments and words. But we are far from loving them really, with vigorous and strong acts that would prove that our love in Christ is not an illusion. "My little children, let us show our love by the true test of action, not by taking phrases on our lips," said St. John (I John 3.18).

We are all familiar with apostasies from Christianity to

Communism, which, in the eyes of their authors, represent a "spiritual conversion," the conversion from the idealistic child to the mature man. They have discovered the concrete dimensions of men, and Christian charity has appeared to them—wrongly so, of course—as an idealistic sentiment with neither root nor truth, a spontaneous refuge for weak consciences that are no longer disturbed by the sight of millions of starving people. The consciousness of these millions of people has become the supreme rule of their thoughts and their actions. And they have rebuilt their system of "values" with reference to this rule. The existing and concrete man, that is the millions of undernourished individuals, of poverty-stricken Chinese, of proletarians from all countries, have become their only true God. All that they have not done for him is "sin," all that they have done that was not for him is deceit and vanity.

Now, we believe that our Lord brings us the same realism, but one founded upon an entirely different base. We know the scene of the Last Judgment (Matt. 25.31), this extraordinary scene we shall never finish thinking about, the scene of the very last judgment of individuals as well as of nations that can have no appeal. And who comes to the bar to accuse or to acquit? Here we see the concrete human masses of the starved, the homeless, the prisoners, the sick. We shall have to endure their look, we shall no longer be able to say that they did not exist, that they were too far away. Our Lord thus affirms that the fundamental rule of ethics, according to which the last judgment will be delivered without appeal, are these brothers with whose misery he identifies himself. Thus, if we must unceasingly remember Christ's presence in us, we must likewise unceasingly recognize his presence in our brothers who are poor. There is no stronger way of uniting the sense of God to the sense of man.

A long time is needed to unite in us this twofold sense. We must, however, aspire to it. Only under this condition will our Christianity be true. A sense of man without a sense of God would find it very difficult to escape despair; the sense of God without the sense of man would no longer be that of the true, revealed God who identified himself with the poor.

We must maintain constantly as one and the same truth, faith in Christ, sole Saviour of the world, and his charity that "compels us." May it impel us to the point of at last loving our brothers truly, "not by phrases on our lips, but by the true test of action."

17 Your Love for One Another Is to Be like the Love I Have Borne You

(John 13.34)

Fraternal love is drawn from the heart of our Lord himself. Indeed, it must take on all the strength and the reality of our own heart of flesh. Yet it springs from a higher source, from the charity of Christ for us. "His love compels me," said St. Paul.

It follows that the shortest road, the only road to true and courageous love of others, is to pass through Christ, to dwell in him. Therefore a new birth is necessary; flesh and blood are not sufficient. We must be born to Christ's manner of loving.

This would be impossible if the Lord himself did not intervene from within. The disciple of Christ is not a superman; he has not "worked himself" to the point of becoming "perfect." He has surrendered himself to Jesus Christ so as to be transformed by him. For this, his faith and his love are more efficacious than his moral efforts, however necessary they may be. And with reference to fraternal love—which contains the whole law and the prophets—he knows very well that he will love as Christ asks him to love only if he remains with Christ's heart: "Your love for one another is to be like the love I have borne you."

In this light, let us see how he loved us.

Humility and gentleness are the most important characteristics of Christ's manner of loving. Here we find the first door to love. "Take my yoke upon yourselves, and learn from me; I am gentle and humble of heart" (Matt. 11.29). Christian love is based upon humility. For it is pride—this love of one's excellence as St. Thomas says— in all its forms, vanity, bitterness, harshness, falling back upon oneself, that makes us oppose one another. To love we must let our heart melt in humility and gentleness.

The washing of the feet is the most significant lesson the Lord taught us about this. Let us not be unmoved by this extraordinary scene. Let us read it in St. John's Gospel. Let us imagine the Lord to whom all glory belongs (I Cor. 2.8) putting a towel about him, pouring water into a basin, and beginning to wash the feet of his disciples. Listen to the great teaching he himself draws from this scene: "I have been setting you an example, which will teach you in turn to do what I have done for you." Let us be careful to note that he wanted to give this teaching at the end of his life, with his Eucharist, as a twofold testament. Then we shall understand that this extraordinary scene cannot simply be an accidental episode in his life, that it is essential to it, and that one cannot be Christian without constantly entering into the spirit of washing the feet of our brothers, for this spirit is his Spirit. It is in the manner of God's loving to lower oneself without ever debasing oneself. What a lesson!

And how our daily experience confirms this! He who never wants to humble himself thus renounces love. Again, humility is the first door to love. Why do we sometimes find it so difficult to love—disunited couples, quarreling families, divided or at least indifferent communities, difficult work relations—if not because pride hardens us in the matter of what we call our "rights" or our different "points of view"? We need but consent to humble ourselves, to recognize our wrongs, and then our hearts loosen. Only true and gentle humility can open hearts.

We enter here into the immense beatitude of the "meek of heart." It takes a long time for this beatitude to appeal to the soul and be recognized for what it really is. It has nothing in common with a sweetish sentimentality or lack of character. It can very well include a certain force, the force dear to our Lord: "The forceful are making the Kingdom of God their prize" (Matt. 11.12), which is proper to generous souls in love with the absolute. Neither does this gentleness suffer compromise with error: "Let your word be Yes for Yes, and No for No" (Matt. 5.37). And the disciple of Christ has the duty of speaking the truth to his brother who is in error, but this force and this courageous presentation of truth must have the supreme power of overcoming all in it which stems from pride or harshness. These souls must always have the gentleness of Christ, as St. Paul tells us, a man of force who yet said of himself: "Here is Paul, making an appeal to you by the gentleness and the courtesy of Christ" (II Cor. 10.1). What is this gentleness of the Gospel made of? There is in it a deep humility and the strength of that love that cannot be confounded. It is expressed by patience, that profound patience which the Gospel declares to be the sign of the truly strong.

Here, as always, we must return to the Heart of Christ. Only he will teach us from within this strength of love that is not discouraged by delays, that is not closed off by ingratitude, that is not vanquished by evil but converts it into gentleness and love. Only the gentle and the humble of heart, converted by the gentle and humble Master, have the strength of love to bear everything and be the victors in the end.

Have you noticed that in his great hymn to charity (I Cor. 13) it is this accent on gentleness and patience that St. Paul mainly develops? Where is true charity to be found? In enthusiasm? In outbursts of feeling? In impulses? Yes, no doubt, but it is found first of all in patience. It is this quality that comes spontaneously to St. Paul's mind when he tries to express its essence: "Charity is patient." In a certain sense, when we have said this, we have said everything. Then "charity sustains, believes, hopes, endures to the last." Its long patience has vanquished everything. St. Theresa of Avila used to say: "Patience obtains everything." What is this patience? It is the strength of love of the gentle and humble of heart. Where do they draw it from? From within themselves? Not at all, they draw it from constant contact with the infinite and ever-present love of Christ, gentle and humble, washing the feet of his disciples. Life's terrible wear and tear neither exhausts nor irritates them, because they "experience" at every instant the soothing gentleness of Christ. And do we, poor Christians, want to learn a little of this patience of Christ? Then let us learn to dwell in his gentle and humble heart.

Forgiveness of injury is related to this. For a long time we think that we have little to forgive and little to be forgiven. Then experience teaches us that forgiveness must be our daily bread in view of the lack of consideration of others, insensitivity, ingratitude, carelessness, deep wounds and real offenses. There are things that hurt us; they enter deep into us and remain there. We may have forgiven with our lips, but our heart did not forgive. The evil did not come out. And that is what this flow of bitterness, these bursts of rebellion which suddenly shake us, express. We have not forgiven. . . . Oh, how powerless we are! Here we must return to the heart of our Lord and in him learn to forgive. He forgave us. He condemned us no more than he condemned the adulterous woman (John

7.53). Shall we not also forgive? Our heart can melt and experience, without any naïveté, the true tears, the sweet tears and the blessed tears that only the gentleness of Christ could bring forth.

The second characteristic of our Lord's "manner" of loving is love for the poor and the little ones. One cannot belong to Christ without sharing this predilection. Here we would like to recall three major texts.

The first concerns the great scene of the Last Judgment (Matt. 25.31). Our Lord teaches us that at this truly last judgment without appeal, the supreme value by which we shall be judged is our attitude toward him as he identifies himself with our brothers in misery. This was already a constant theme in the psalms and the prophecies, that the Lord comes to the defense of the poor man who is so much abused in the world. And Christ came in person, in the name of his Father, to take this prerogative of God for his own. From now on, the poor will be his concern. One can no longer touch them without touching him.

Who are they, these poor and little ones? The Gospel names them: They are those compelled by the most elementary needs, they are the strangers far away from their country, they are those who have no support in the world, widows, orphans. To me the poor man is that one of my brothers who is in need and who finds himself in my path in such a way that I would have to take another road in order not to meet him. At this moment is there not for each of us one of Christ's poor to assist? And what is he in want of? Not always of money; it may be affection, attention, a fraternal heart.

The second text is the one where our Lord answers the envoys of John the Baptist (Luke 7.22). One of the signs that the messianic times have come is the fact that the poor are having the Gospel preached to them. Thus the sign of the Messiah is the evangelization of the poor. And what shall we understand by evangelization? That they have heard the good tidings, that they have understood that God had not abandoned them, but that they are his people, that the poor and the little ones so easily despised by the world are indeed the people of God. If the poor were taken away from the Church, the principal part of her would be lacking. Is it not great cause for suffering that the human masses no longer expect their deliverance from the Church of Christ? Even Christ has been taken from them.

A third characteristic of the manner of our Lord's loving is to love us even to the Cross. Blessed Jordan of Saxony, immediate successor to St. Dominic, tells us that the saint prayed to God "to give him the true charity that lead Christ to the Cross." It is such a love that we receive from Christ. Here we have the decisive criterion of fraternal love. Does it give us the strength to suffer for our brothers, and to suffer very much if necessary? The soul often has the impression that it is bereft of this true charity. We love our brothers because of a natural affinity, because we "love to love," because we find "consolation" in our devotion. Basically, we love those who love us, but the charity that comes from Christ has us love even to the Cross those even who do not love us.

Our Lord said: "This is the greatest love a man can show, that he should lay down his life for his friends" (John 16.3). And St. John speaks of the practical application of this in his First Epistle: "God has proved his love to us by laying down his life for our sakes" (I John 3.16). The love coming from Christ goes that far, and it is this love that we received at baptism. It is truly a question of giving our life, of loosing our life, of being worn out by work. Work, labor, worries, all this is included in fraternal love, if it truly comes from Christ. We could say that it is a love that would have us undertake anything. Let us simply remember the journeyings, the fatigues, the worries, and the wear and tear of the saints. They bore their brothers' burden. And a burden that does not weigh heavily is not a burden at all.

St. Paul tells us simply: "Bear the burden of one another's failings; then you will be fulfilling the law of Christ" (Gal. 6.2). Very few formulas are as luminous and as simplifying. Thus the law of Christ is accomplished—nothing more comes after that—when we bear one another's burden. Do we have the generosity to carry the other's burden when our own is already heavy? And yet, what simplicity and what joy: "Bear the burden—all burdens of one another." What Christian can fail to understand this?

The more we meditate upon these texts, the more we realize that we are very far from having even a little of this fraternal charity that brought Christ to the Cross. Do we have as much as a mustard seed? And yet, however poor we are, great is our hope since the Lord himself wants to teach us to love as he loves: "Your love for one another is to be like the love I have borne you."

18 Blessed Are You Who Are Poor: The Kingdom of God Is Yours

(Luke 6.20)

Let this amazing new word enter into us. Let us receive it with an open soul and with the attitude of a man wanting to be a disciple of Christ.

Let us receive it, even if we do not understand it. In advance let us decide in its favor, even against ourselves. It will find its way into us during the course of our life. When we were children we did not pay much attention to it, or we listened to it as to one of those sublime maxims that exalt us without affecting our lives. Now that we are men, we must learn from it. A lifetime will not be long enough to become converted by it. But the stakes are worth it: It is a question of taking part in the beatitude promised by Christ, and having access to his Kingdom.

However, let us make clear from the beginning that we shall not be able to understand this word, if the Lord himself does not teach us in the depth of our heart with this accent by which his sheep recognize him: "Blessed are you who are poor: The Kingdom of God is yours."

Meaning of evangelical poverty

The doctrine of our Lord on poverty does not present itself directly as a social doctrine. Indeed, like the whole Gospel, it teaches us first a certain interior attitude that we must have with reference to riches. This does not mean that it is lacking efficiency and realism. If it is real, it will cause a change in our life, and will inspire a social doctrine that men will adopt little by little. But it first involves a conversion of the heart.

Moreover, by riches, we must understand, according to the Gospel, all kinds of riches: material and spiritual. Indeed, with its divine realism, the Gospel mainly underlines the use of the first kind, and it even emphasizes the most elementary riches: bread, clothing, shelter. It is, first of all, in this area that we must assume a Christian attitude with reference to worldly goods; this keeps us in contact with the earthly realities. Every doctrine on poverty that avoids them would soon reduce itself to an inconsistent and inefficient idealism, an easy refuge for our slight desires, but not at all related to the world of men of goodwill. This being clear, we must understand that the teaching of Christ refers also to riches other than material goods: our spiritual riches—our intelligence, our culture, our talents, our heart, our character, our "good conscience" even. Here again, here particularly, we must be poor, true poor of Christ, who do not depend upon these riches for they would soon become unjust.

We may now distinguish three directions in which to find the sense of evangelical poverty. In short, our Lord says to us: "Your true riches do not consist in your material goods, not even in your jealously kept spiritual goods; they are found in the love of the Father in heaven. Keep your treasure in heaven. To be poor, according to my spirit, is to have placed your treasure in the love of God." He also says: "To be poor is to trust in the providence of God, in the concern that I have for each one of you." Finally, he says to us: "To be poor is to imitate me. But I was born in a manger for animals like a little wretch. I died on the Cross, stripped of my clothes. Nevertheless, like me you must rise above hardships and strive to improve your own way of life and that of others."

—To place one's treasure in heaven;

—To trust in divine providence;

—To accept the conditions of life and yet to attempt to rise above them.

These are the three intentions that the soul who wishes to become poor according to Christ aims at. They can never be dissociated, although the soul may emphasize one or the other according to its vocation. We shall now examine them, one after the other.

To put one's treasure in heaven

Our Lord, seriously and mercifully, calls our attention to the quality of the goods we seek: "Where your treasure-house is, there your heart is too" (Matt. 6.19). Where have you placed your treasure? In perishable goods or in the only good that does not perish, that is placing yourself peacefully into the hands of God? This is the very serious question which we must answer.

Now, our Lord knows very well, alas, that a great number of people are attracted, fascinated and finally led astray by the lure of material goods (or even by spiritual goods jealously kept for themselves). They have placed their treasure in these goods which they consider, not as a legitimate means for living, but as an immoderate enlarging of their own personality. These goods have been, for example, acres of land, automobiles, businesses, titles in the bank, standards of living; and in the same proportion, the Kingdom of God, its truth, its justice, its love, have disappeared from their eyes. The "realists" even declare that "it" does not exist. We must recall here the moaning of Christ seeing so many souls who have falsified their own nature and have gradually become "materialized": "The cares of this world and the deceitfulness of riches and their other appetites smother the word, so that it remains fruitless" (Mark 4.19). They have become almost insensitive to spiritual goods. Mammon has become their master. God preserve them from being but dried wood! And our Lord seems to say to his disciples: You also, be careful not to let material goods close your heart and overpower you. Nothing is more easy and more treacherous. But keep your heart open to true richness, which is my true love for you and your own. May you only understand that.

"To be rich" means to put one's trust in one's own riches and not in the help of God. Here, we touch on the very root of spiritual poverty according to Christ, or, conversely, of evil richness. He is poor, according to Christ, who trusts in God; he is rich, in the manner cursed by Christ, who puts his trust (in the strong sense) in his riches. Little by little, the rich reach this extreme of evil that consists in not needing God any longer. How could God possibly reach such people? Human sufficiency, pride of life, as St. John says, have blinded them on all sides. The "rich" man, with reputation, friends, several automobiles, is so sure of himself and his works! Another man who has been successful in everything—academic work, competition, marriage, children—how difficult it is for him not to depend on himself, his intelligence, his work, his good conduct! Another man, who has succeeded in controlling himself, in dominating the flesh and vulgarity, who enjoys the testimony of a good conscience, how easily he can become a pharisee, rich with himself and yet lacking the only true richness! None of these people are poor according to Jesus. They are not without this last richness, the most dangerous one, that which clings most strongly to our "self": *confidence* in their own riches, immoderate esteem of themselves. But he who has experienced unemployment, sickness of his wife and children, temptation, his own weakness, he who has begun to take recourse in God and to trust his mercy, he has begun to become poor, and the Kingdom of God, of Christ, has opened itself to him.

And this is so, because our true richness lies in the gratuitous and merciful love of God for us, and because in order to receive it, we must begin by not putting our treasure and our strength in ourselves any longer. In this sense, we can say that the specific virtue of the evangelical poor is hope, in as far as it teaches us to expect everything from God with an intrepid joy and a humble assurance.

All these things shall be yours without the asking

We can now see more clearly what interior attitude we should have with reference to earthly goods (even spiritual goods). We must, first of all, have put our treasure in God's love. There is our true wealth. Our Lord expresses it in a phrase which shines forth like a luminous light: "Make it your first care to find the Kingdom of God and his approval" (Matt. 6.33; Luke 12.31). If you seek this out first, everything is put in the right order. If you do not make it your first care, you condemn yourself to being unable to discern things. The Kingdom of God and his approval (justice) are the truth that will deliver your soul. This means that we must, first of all, bring ourselves in harmony with God, considering this the greatest good, incomparably the greatest. For yourself, for your wife, your children, for those you love, do you really desire the greatest good? And do you desire it for itself, and not in order to have peace or security for eternal life, for then you would subtly consider your own peace and eternal security as your greatest good (and you would still be rich)? Or do you desire it because it is the good of God which you want and love for his sake? If this is your first care, then you have begun to be poor. Your true wealth is in the hands of God.

When our basic attitude has been established, our Lord promises us more: "And all other things shall be yours without the asking," that is if you have not asked for it, if it has not been your first care.

And what are these things? "Your Father knows well what you need" (Luke 12.30). First we need daily bread, in a broad sense, the subsistence necessary for our homes, for the education of our children. In our day, how many fathers and mothers of families must stake their lives on the word of Christ? With what intrepidity they must believe in his promise? They are learning—and it is always difficult—evangelical poverty. They rejoin, in their turn, the long line of witnesses, of humble servants of God, good workers, who say simply at the end of their life: "We did not lack bread."

And sometimes, most often even, God sends something

additional, unexpected, unhoped for, in his divine delicacy. Let us look at our own lives. Who among us has never witnessed this delicacy of God toward him? It is the word of the Lord at the end of his life: "Did you go in want of anything, when I sent you without purse, or wallet, or shoes? They told him, nothing" (Luke 22.35). He who has learned to trust in God, to stake his life on him, experiences this law of "things given without the asking"; let us add that he also learns to give thanks. To thank is proper to the poor. The rich do not even think of it, so surprised are they to be lacking anything. But the poor love to give thanks. It is an authentic part of the evangelical poverty to thank God for our meals, for each of our joys. Our little children can thus learn, without even realizing it, to enter the beatitude of Christ. They will also learn to trust in God more than in themselves.

How dear to God this attitude is! Was it not the life of Mary and Joseph in Nazareth? Their true wealth was in the love of the Father, their true strength in hope.

One fruit of this filial abandonment in the hands of God in heaven, will be holy joy and freedom of the heart. Let us not be mistaken: There we find, partly, the secret of the Franciscan joy which attracts every Christian so powerfully. When we read the texts and bring to life again the extraordinary origins of the Franciscan movement, when we inhale the scent that emanates from St. Francis and St. Clare, we cannot doubt that their joy was due to poverty. Indeed, they have experienced a painful indigence, but at the same time an authentic, smiling joy, taking its source in the total surrender of their self to God. To be the poor one of God is to entrust oneself, with Jesus, to his Father. God nourishes the poor who entrust themselves to him. And his own poor experience thus the joy of depending upon him.

To advance the social condition

But does not such an attitude eliminate all effort to work one's way up, to improve one's social condition, to plan for a better life than our own for our children? And, on a broader scale, how will such an attitude give rise to economic progress? Will it not mean leaving the way open to "the children of the world who are more prudent after their own fashion than the children of light" (Luke 16.8)? We do not underrate the seriousness of this problem submitted to the Christian conscience.

Let us simply indicate here in what direction we should keep searching. Evangelical poverty cannot oppose itself to magnanimity and audacity, that is, to that quality of the soul which consists in seeing and accomplishing things boldly. It will be our duty to improve our social condition when this condition deprives us of the spiritual freedom needed by ourselves and our family. Also, money is no evil in itself. It can be an extraordinary tool for the good.

In fact, it is always necessary, at least at a given time, for the flowering of the works of God. The saints who had to maintain hospitals and schools knew it very well. In certain cases it will even be necessary to become rich, but one realizes immediately the profound orientation which changes everything: One will have to be rich for God, not for oneself. The aim of the soul lies not in the extension of one's own personality. It is oriented in one way or another toward serving God better.

It may be the task of our generation to show a new face of evangelical poverty, and, in this century eager to acquire everything, to show that the sons of light can assume even wealth while remaining poor spiritually. Employers, manufacturers, captains of industries and commerce, can thus, with the grace of God, make use of the "unjust wealth" for God's Glory (Luke 16.9). But the task will be arduous and will always require a complete integrity of the heart, proportioned to the difficulty. "What are you searching for? Where did you place your treasure?" And let us dare say it, God will always mercifully allow that, owing to the force of circumstances, we belong to those little ones who will finally have to turn with confidence to the Father in heaven and ask him for their daily bread. And blessed shall we be.

19 The Poor Have the Gospel Preached to Them

(Luke 7.22)

To be poor according to Christ, is to have found and placed one's treasure in God's love for us. There lies our infinite richness. If we have discovered this, our heart is rectified with respect to worldly goods, it is detached. Moreover, we have understood that our strength consists in being in God's hands, truly relying on him and expecting everything from him: daily bread, daily grace, daily forgiveness. Such are the poor according to Christ.

And yet we must go farther. With a realism that will never penetrate us enough, Christ ties poverty to fraternal charity. If he asks his disciples to be poor, it is because there are poor to love and to help. To love poverty is, in fact, to love the poor. Let us consider this thought seriously and honestly: I am a disciple of Christ only if, in total truth, I have a friend, I have friends among the poor. Only in this way will we be able to appreciate the real purpose of Christ's coming into the world, that is to minister to the needs and wants of every man.

Blessed is he who has an understanding of the poor

The poor man is indeed a true mystery. Natural sympathy is not sufficient to penetrate him. We must be impregnated by the Spirit of Christ. The sense of Christ and the intimate sense of the poor are tied together. The psalm already said: "Blessed is he who takes thought for the poor and destitute" (Psalm 40). It is a blessing to be endowed with this understanding. He who has received it is not far from the Kingdom of God.

In the Old Testament the "poor" were the social class who did not benefit from the consideration given to high birth, wealth, power, even education. For this reason, they were more or less despised and considered people of no account. They were often even the victims of hard masters and rapacious creditors. Those who have nothing to make themselves respected, how easily they are abused! Whom can they ask for justice? We see in Scripture this often repeated assertion: It is God who will take their defense. They are his recognized clients; they are his friends. And he, he is their refuge, their justice, their support. This is one of the most constant themes of the Prophets and the Psalms.

When Christ comes, it is to them that he speaks first. His astonishing beatitudes refer to them in the first place. The poor, the gentle, the sorrowful, belong with slight differences to the same social category. Our Lord also uses another strangely enlightening word to designate them. He calls them the "little ones," those who cannot defend themselves very well in society. And they are his brothers, "his own brothers" (Matt. 25.40). Let us note this fact very carefully. God has aligned himself on their side.

For it is this which is amazing. God, Christ, visits us through them. In a major scene in the Gospel, Christ warns us solemnly that he identifies himself with them. It is even on this basis, on our attitude toward them and by the same token toward him, that the world (all nations) will be judged. Here again, let us weigh these words. The last judgment of the world, which will be without appeal, will depend on the world's attitude toward the poor, that is toward Christ identified with them. For, "I was hungry and you gave me food. . . . Believe me, when you did it to one of the least of my brethren here, you did it to me" (Matt. 25.40). The poor, the little one, is thus consecrated the Sacrament of Christ. If we do not have, at least in some way, the sense of the poor, we should ask ourselves with concern whether we have the sense of Christ.

Another word of our Lord casts light upon this mystery of the poor. When John the Baptist asks from his prison if he is the "one who is to come" or if another should be expected, he has two of his disciples answer that "the blind see and the lame walk," and he finishes with the great news: "the poor have the Gospel preached to them." Thus the messianic era is inaugurated with the evangelization of the poor. And what is this evangelization? It is that they have received the good tidings. What tidings? That they are loved; yes, loved by the Father who is in heaven and who has given to them—to them especially—the Messiah who is his Son. Yes, the poor (those who are despised, scoffed at, considered unimportant) come to believe that they are loved for themselves. Then they are evangelized and the Lord is not far away. He is "He who is to come." It is at this sign that in his prison John the Baptist realizes that the Kingdom of Heaven will begin on earth. In the same manner, without any illuminism, we can, we must understand that the evangelization of the poor, that is the revelation to them of the love of the Father in heaven through the love of his disciples, hastens the coming of the Son of Man. Where the poor are evangelized, Christ is not far away. This is the dawn of the Kingdom of God on earth. To look at it another way, should not this be the great scandal that should burn our hearts, viz., that the people of the twentieth century no longer expect their hope from Christ, indeed not because of him, but because of our lack of interest?

We shall have this understanding of the poor only if the spirit of our Lord penetrates us little by little. Without this intimate realization, fruit in us of grace and of constant association with Christ, we shall remain tragically indifferent to the mystery of the poor, without realizing that we are thus passing by Christ without recognizing him. For, although he no longer visits us in his personal, historical Incarnation, he has not left us yet. He continues to live among us through and in the poor. At every moment, we are being judged by the very attitude we have toward them, that is to say toward him: "It is to me that you did not do it."

In practice, it is difficult to recognize the poor. If the intimate sense of the poor that Christ gives us is unique, it is not completely mysterious. We also need a more human virtue called prudence. There are nuisances, beggars, whom misery, alas, has made into liars and evil persons. There is, especially, the innumerable crowd of those for whom we can do nothing or very little, even if we had a hundred lives and great resources. The difficult question then is to know, who are for me the poor of Christ? Let us examine this very carefully, for it is an important matter. All of us have a poor (poors) of Christ in our life, and we cannot ignore them. We suggest the following practical conclusion to be meditated by each: For me the poor of Christ is this "little one" who needs me and who finds himself on my path, in such a way that I would have to take a byway in order to avoid him. Thus the man who had fallen into the hands of thieves and was lying on the roadside was on the road of the priest and the Levite who proceeded onward. But the Samaritan stopped and it was Christ whom he mounted upon his beast. May

Gospel Spirituality

God give us the understanding of the poor man who finds himself on our path, and who may be largely in want of our attention and our love.

Receiving the poor

We must then receive such a poor one. This means that we must open our heart to him. Our Lord appeals directly to this center of ourselves, and the poor will make no mistake about it. It is not necessarily a question of a movement of our sensitivity which we are unable to bring about or which may even be too easy. It will have to be an act of true charity, "without pretense" says St. Paul, of true concern, of deep and authentic care. For, if I do not give the poor man my love, how will he be evangelized, that is to say, how will he perceive through me and without my talking, that he is an object of love for his own sake, on the part of the Father who is in heaven? The true poor of Christ must give his love. Thus everything will be taken from him. He will be truly poor and yet he will enrich many, as St. Paul reminds us. And it is this language only that the poor will understand.

In one sense, everything would be won if we had truly given our heart. But more concrete suggestions may be helpful here.

The following is taken not from the letter of the Gospel, but from its spirit. It could be expressed thus: Receive the "little one" even better than the "great one." And if a precedence should be established, it should be in favor of the poor. Here again, let us weigh these words. If someone has to wait in a waiting room, for a visit, for a letter to be written, we must not let the poor wait. And by poor we understand the child who appears ungrateful, the sick friend expecting a visit for which I feel no eagerness, the group of people who seem less brilliant than another. I must endeavor every day to receive the poor even better than the rich. Then I shall be of the Spirit of Christ.

And here is another formula, taken this time from the very letter of the Gospel: "If a man would borrow from you, do not turn away" (Matt. 5.42). Let us exclude, right away, the nuisances, but if we take this statement as a practical rule, we shall be surprised by all the light it will give us. He who wants to borrow from us, is our brother whom God places in our path. And what does he want to borrow? Not always money . . . more often, our time, and always, in any case, some of our attention and our love. And who can pride himself in never having avoided such borrowers? Discernment indeed is needed; we must know how to close our door, for instance, in the very name of a better charity (safeguarding hours of study and of indispensable silence). But the evangelical word remains true, and we must let it enter us with all its strength: "Do not turn away from a man who would borrow from you." How far this word goes in us, and how we realize that of our own accord we can neither understand nor follow it! Only the interior presence of Christ can accomplish that.

To share the life of the poor

And yet, merely to receive the poor man is not sufficient. We must help him effectively, and do it with such nobility and truth that he does not feel humiliated to have to receive it. We must, first of all, really help him. Here, the disciple of Christ must not fear to be where this help is vital. Social justice, social service, social security, so many words which have become symbols, and yet we must discover without prejudice—beyond the symbols and the excesses—a true reality that Christ takes into account and that is a true help to our brothers. However, one condition is necessary: that the true gentleness of Charity impregnate all the anonymity and coolness that these words might contain. Even if social justice was to help all cases, there will always be poor ones, unfortunately, that is beings who are not objects of love for their own sake. They will always need to be evangelized, that is to be loved. Hospitals, nurseries, dispensaries, social services, the charity of Christ must impregnate them all continually, at the same time as their techniques, which are quite necessary, are being improved.

And that is probably why, in spite of our mediocrity, we feel instinctively that we have not done anything to help our brothers, the poor, as long as we have not shared their life. This is the feeling of many admirable priests and lay people who are motivated by the love of Christ and of their brothers who are poor. They finally decide to share the same inhuman work, the same poor lodgings, the same common hospital ward; also the same joys and the same simplicity of the heart. It is not a questionable proselytism that thus impels them. It is much more. It is the love of Christ who loved the poor.

Blessed are we if one day the Spirit of Jesus, authentically recognized, leads us this far. But, in the meantime, we too can truly share the life of the poor. First of all, if we belong to them. And we all belong to them somehow: insecurity for the future, worries, difficult payments to meet. How we must call to God with confidence! Then, if we accept with joy the privations that life brings us or that we impose on ourselves, under the condition that we alone bear them, and not our children or our wife: more simple food, less smoking or drinking, a smaller apartment, a delayed trip, etc. . . . How can we not be happy to lack something since through this we communicate a little with the universal distress of the poor and with Christ? The "realists" will say that the poor are scarcely aided by our efforts, or even ridiculously so, but we know that in the eyes of Christ our efforts have immense importance, and in a sense this is everything. For in our way we are actually *communicating* with our poor brothers and also with

Christ. We do not lie, therefore, when we say that we *love* them.

In this sense we shall deprive ourselves of something. Of our superfluity, first of all. Indeed, it is difficult to evaluate it. The necessary, in fact, can include a minimum of security for the future and of social improvement for ourselves and our children. We even think that only an intimate and faithful sense of Christ can help us discern what our superfluity is. Timorous and scrupulous souls will have to ask for the advice of the sane and vigorous. But we must all ask Christ to give us his light in order to recognize this superfluity and give it up for the benefit of the poor of God.

There will be cases when we must even give from that which is necessary to us. We all remember the story of the widow's mite (Mark 12.14). Let us read it again. It will certainly move us. Priests of Christ can witness that the evangelical story continues and that they often live from the widow's mite. And with what respect do they receive this mite given to Christ? But we, can we not sometimes give some of our "necessary things," that which we find difficult to give up, a dress, a book, a trip? Let us try, and perhaps as in the mysterious kiss of St. Francis to the leper, we shall find so much joy that we shall gain a little understanding of the Beatitude of the Poor.

20 *The Son of Man Has Nowhere to Lay His Head*

(Luke 9.58)

An abandonment full of faith and courage into the hands of the Father who is in heaven, an effective love for the poor,* such are the spiritual roots of evangelical poverty. But our Lord gives us a third lesson: He wanted to be poor even to the point of destitution. We too must, with his grace, reach this point. It is not possible to be poor according to the Gospel without looking often at Christ in his crib or on the Cross. There are even extremes of distress where any other food is unbearable. It is for these moments especially that the following remarks were intended.

The imitation of Christ

At all times, the imitation of Christ has been the essential incentive of a truly Christian soul. It has often been said, but we must repeat it: Christianity is Christ. Nothing has been done as long as no personal relationship unites the Christian to his Lord, known as a loved Person to whom

* Cf. chap. 18. 19.

one can give one's faith. We know the words of St. Paul: "As for me, to live is Christ." Let us say them very simply, in spite of our misery; they also must be our essential aspiration. And therefore, Christ must become our love: "O my soul, is Christ your love, your living strength, your intimate sap?"

But if this love is true, it cannot do without imitation. The question is not only to meet the Person of Jesus, we must let ourselves be transformed by it. It is through his Spirit that we belong to him. He told us in the Gospel that it mattered little to be of his family according to the flesh, if one was not of it according to the spirit. Only under this condition are we his brother, his sister or his mother (Matt. 12.46). So it is with us; it matters little that we have the sense of Christ if we are not transformed by him. We must be found true to his Spirit.

Moreover, we must not conceive this imitation of the Lord in the manner of an artist copying a model external to him. Such imitation would not go very far and would be but a dead work. We can imitate Christ only because he is in us and because his grace, like an intimate sap, renews us from inside. He is speaking to us in his Gospel, and we must listen to him with all the attention of our intelligence and our love. And let us not forget, the Christ of the Gospel is not among the dead. He is alive. He is in us. He is, at the same time, he who transforms us and our divine model. His example is not external to us. It is an intimate experience. He is a call in us, an attraction, an exigency, and he is at the same time Light and Strength.

Let us consider the history of the Church. All Christian renewals were born from an imitation of Christ understood in this manner. The saints only wanted to be "his original but incomplete continuators," as Bergson remarked. "Him I would learn to know" said St. Paul (Philippians 3.30), and all the saints repeated this cry: to know him in his mercy or in his truth, in his gentleness or in his poverty. And how can we know him thus if not by imitating him? His loved Person has brought about this miracle. It is in this light that we must finally see the extraordinary attraction of his poverty for so many souls. "I love poverty because he loved it," Pascal stated. Outside of this active love for Christ, there can only be pale imitations, but no authentic saints.

Christ in his destitution

Christ wanted to experience poverty to the point of destitution. Let us dwell upon these extraordinary words and penetrate them.

We do not see in the Gospel that our Lord lived habitually a life of destitution. The Holy Family in Nazareth, the Lord in his apostolic ministry, seem to have known poverty, but not misery—at least not as an habitual state. We know the great difference there is between these two realities. Misery is to lack the necessities. It very often leads to sin or at least provokes an alienation of the soul which opposes itself to the Kingdom of God. When the actual hunger for daily bread grips the heart too intensely, it is no longer possible, at least as a general rule, to go freely to God. Our Lord did not beatify such misery and he obliges us to fight it. Poverty, on the contrary, consists in a moderation, which gives us daily bread, but obliges us to rely on God for the following day. It seems that this was the way of living of the Holy Family and of our Lord. From a social point of view, they were humble people, but not destitute. Joseph earned his bread with the work of his hands, and the Lord himself did likewise. Thus, God-made-man wanted to live and hide his greatness in the ordinary.

And yet, the fact remains that Christ wanted to experience poverty to the point of destitution, at least at two major moments of his life: his birth and his death. On our earth the little children of the poor ordinarily have at least a cradle to receive them at birth. God-made-man wanted to be born "in a manger, because there was no room for them in the inn" (Luke 2.7). Need we comment upon these extraordinary words of the revealed text? Either all this is but a tale, or we must take it seriously at last. And likewise, when he dies, God-made-man again chooses destitution. He is stripped of his clothes, abandoned by his friends, separated from his mother, rejected by the religious hierarchy of his people, totally poor and alone. He does not even feel any longer, unless in the innermost part of his human soul, the presence of his Father, who has not abandoned him. Here again, we must not get too accustomed to hearing these amazing things, so that familiarity prevents us from pondering them at great length as St. Dominic, St. Francis of Assisi and Father Chevrier did. They suffered and considered themselves as liars as long as the Lord had not called them to share his destitution. All other nourishment seemed tasteless to them.

As for us, poor disciples of Christ, these heights frighten us. And yet do we not, all of us, have some access to them? Do we not find among us a father out of work who cannot feed his family? A mother whose strength is diminishing while her children are still small? An old man without means? Is there no distress for someone? The destitution of Christ continues on earth. At such moments we can only cling silently to the Cross where we find our Lord and his Mother. He wanted to experience this himself. He knows our distress. Will he not come to our rescue? And the last word he spoke on earth, before his death, is a word of abandonment: "Father, into thy hands I commend my spirit."

To be poor according to Christ, is to go that far.

In this connection, the witnesses for the canonization of St. Dominic tell us that his face was particularly joyful whenever he was in adversity. And St. Francis of Assisi tells us where "perfect joy" lies. We must read again this extraordinary passage of the *Fioretti*, not as an act of bravery, or a poetic creation, but as the testimony of a man who found his joy in sharing the destitution of Christ.

As for us, we shall be able to reach these heights at rare moments only. Let us leave it to our Father in heaven to apportion to us our hours of distress. But could we not accustom ourselves to be happy when we lack something? With her habitual realism the little Saint of Lisieux had realized this: "To be poor," she said, "is to be happy to lack something."

It is not he who says: Lord, Lord . . .

What shall we say, after these considerations? Should we not rather keep silent and confess that we resemble very little those poor whom the Lord has blessed? And yet, let us have the courage to formulate the three following conclusions for ourselves:

1) To be poor is to abandon myself into the hands of God, when I have finished my work. Exaggerated worries, gnawing cares, overwhelming anxieties mean that I do not rely enough on God. No doubt it is impossible to avoid anguish at certain times. God himself does not reproach us. And yet, our anguish must become appeased in him. In many cases I must reproach myself for my worries that precede events; they amount to a lack of faith and love.

Sufficient unto the day is the evil thereof. Work, suffer, and silently entrust yourself to God.

2) To be poor is also to share what I have. Here we find, we think, the crucial point of poverty, where we must gain complete victory, failing which we shall always remain triflers. We know the advice given by John the Baptist to those who came to him to be baptized: "The man who has two coats must share with the man who has none; and the man who has food to eat must do the like" (Luke 3.11). These words are from the Gospel. Listen to their sound. Simple men, those whom we mean when we say "the people," understand them directly. Do not soften them at any price. Consider the matter. Have you nothing to share? Clothes, meals, lodging, services? No doubt discernment is needed, you will not do it every day. But on this point we must overcome ourselves if we truly want to be poor like Christ. Open your heart, and also your home, and learn to share with those (even members of your family) who are in need.

3) To be poor, finally, will consist in welcoming with joy all inconveniences or privations as long as they are personal: worn clothes which could need replacing, useful equipment, books we must do without, and tempting trips that are too expensive for my budget. All that is my daily bread I must learn to receive with joy. And maybe one day, Christ will judge me worthy of sharing his destitution. We must not wish it, it would be presumptuous. But we

can, at least, keep our heart available for everything that he will want. Heroism is rarely improvised.

All this is included in the true love of Christ and his poor. Aim at this love, and, from this living germ, the true poverty of Christ will be given to you little by little.

21 It Is Fire That I Have Come to Spread over the Earth
(Luke 12.49)

How we must ask to be set ablaze by this fire! This is because missionary zeal is indispensable to the Church. Mission, or God sending forth his messengers, is a divine and permanent reality founding the Church at every instant. No Christian can consider himself outside of this great flow of witnesses of God. Are we consumed at all by this fire?

First we must know where to find it. In ourselves? Unfortunately, we are so cold and timid. Like the prophet Jeremias, we are rather inclined to say: "I am but a child and I know not how to speak." We also know that if it is relatively easy to start something, it is much more difficult to last through to the end; we know that "human soil" is unprofitable and heavy to plow. Indeed, if it was left to ourselves, we would not go very far. In order to open our heart to the immense breath of the Kingdom of God, to set ablaze in us a fire that cannot be quenched, we must go to Another with whom we must be united unceasingly in humility and silence, with strength and fidelity.

Then we shall learn from him that it is his will to send us into the world. There is in Christ, we can say with assurance, a will to send us into the world. And we must let resound in us with intrepidity and courage this sending message. Listen to it and once more let it vanquish and convert you. Once more, the Lord does not speak in trifles. The saints believed his words in earnest. And these words burned and consumed them. Let us listen with them.

"It is fire that I have come to spread over the earth, and what better wish can I have than that it should be kindled?" (Luke 12.49). Here we have the fire that must burn us! It is the very fire that consumed the heart of Christ, it is a fire that is not from the earth; it is a fire coming from God, the fire of his Holy Spirit of Love in whom we have all been baptized. It is the will of God that something burn in us and hurt us. We have met men whom we felt were being consumed by something that was not from the earth: hunger and thirst for justice, mercy, expectation of God. They set a fire ablaze in us. St. Dominic must have been one of them. As he spoke, the hearts of his listeners would be set ablaze. But in order not to quench this fire, he prayed at length during the night, while those who had listened to him were sleeping. The fire of God then burned him and hurt him. For he was in contact with Christ, with him who had said that he had come to spread fire over the earth. And as for us, poor Christians with cold hearts, we must humbly ask God: "Set something ablaze in my heart, something true, something that nothing can quench: neither failure, nor age, nor tiredness; something humble and gentle; something coming from you."

"I came upon an errand from my Father, and now I am sending you out in my turn" (John 20.21; 17.18). Thus we are caught in a divine flow. There is but one sending, one mission: that in which the Father sends his Son, and we in turn are included in this sending, in our lowly but real place.* Christ sends us in the living breath of his Holy Spirit. Thus we did not set out of our own accord; we are not speaking of our own accord. The Lord is sending us, it is he who says: "Do not be afraid, speak out, for I have a great following in this city" (Acts 18.9). We may regret the silence of a cloister: "O blissful solitude, only beatitude," sings the Cistercian soul. However, at the same time, we must listen to another call: Christ must be announced. We must follow this call. There is nothing to be regretted. If it is Christ who is sending us, our holiness will consist in being consumed by his mission. This mission is not exterior to us. It compels us incessantly from within. To surrender to it is to surrender to Christ.

"Go out all over the world, and preach the Gospel to the whole of creation" (Mark 16.15). We must be there where God placed us, in our family, our situation in life.

* We must emphasize here—it is also emphasized in the Gospel—that the mission of Christ is not entrusted only to the hierarchical Church and those sent by the Church, but to all men.

We must not escape from it. The saints taught us that only faithfulness to the present moment, the duty of this moment, was the preparation for the future. We contribute to the progress of the reign of God only by holding our place faithfully, the place that nobody else could fill. At the same time, however, we must always keep our soul open to what God holds in store for us. St. Dominic devoted himself completely to the foundation of his Order. At the same time he listened in his soul to the mysterious Cumans about whom he thought throughout his whole life. While it is precise and humble, the missionary call is universal from the beginning. I am sent to my brother who is my neighbor, and yet I must always think of the farthest of my brothers. The whole world must be won, yet I must concentrate my attention upon the small province of my own efforts and the fervor of my love. I must be haunted by these immense regions that the Gospel has not penetrated, such as in Asia and Africa. And at the same time I must realize that the only thing God asks from me and that nobody could do in my place is that I devote myself to the education of my children, that I conduct my business with integrity, that I teach catechism to the local children. But, while carrying out these ordinary duties, I must also carry in me and nourish the thought of the mysterious Cumans.

"Yet still, when he looked at the multitude, he was moved with pity for them, seeing them harried and abject, like sheep that have no shepherd" (Matt. 9.36). The missionary flame lights itself at the heart of Christ; it is kindled also in the direct contact of the light of men. The more realistic awareness of the condition of the present world may be one of the authentic signs of the missionary vocation of today. There is a courage, a will to see clearly, a refusal to accept illusions and false consolations, that come from Christ. Moreover, there is not one great apostle who did not have this burning flame together with great lucidity, who did not know from the beginning that things would be tough, that he was engaging in a fierce battle. A sensitive heart is not sufficient to become an apostle.

But what does this flame consist of? What is the object of the mission? Here the revealed words introduce us into a true mystery: The object of the Christian mission is the manifestation of the Love of God.

Listen to our Lord: "I have made thy name known to the men whom thou hast entrusted to me, chosen out of the world" (John 17.6). This name of God, sacred and very gentle, was hidden and is still hidden for whoever is not reborn from water and the Spirit. The Name of God is he himself; it is his infinite and very close reality. As long as we do not know him—heart to heart—we have no God on earth; there has been no revelation of God for us. Christ is precisely he who has revealed the name of his Father. He has revealed to us the secret of his unique, immense love:

He loved men and he wanted to be loved by them. Here are the good tidings: A poor human heart has received the Kingdom of God. God has revealed his Name, his true nature to a poor human heart. This poor man is then evangelized, he is no longer an orphan. He can glorify God and sanctify his Name, this new Name which will be his whole life in proportion as God reigns in it. The world does not know it, but it was Christ's desire that he should know it: "I have revealed, and will reveal, thy name to them; so that the love thou hast bestowed upon me may dwell in them, and I too may dwell in them." Could anything stronger be said?

Let us listen to St. John, directly echoing the words of the Lord: "What has revealed the love of God, is that he has sent his only begotten Son into the world so that we might have life through him." Thus the sending of Christ, the Christian mission, is truly the revelation of the love of God, the revelation of something that was hidden up to that point, and that remains hidden as long as we have not been "evangelized." That is, it remains an incomprehensible love of God, so incomprehensible that the first Christian generation had to create a new word, *Agape*, to designate it. Only then is the Name of God revealed.

Evangelization, as we see it, comprises two planes: There is the exterior announcement of Christ and there is the revelation to the soul's eyes of the unfathomable love of God, of which Christ is the living proof. That is to say that evangelization is a mystery in the truest sense of the word, and not the result of tricks and special techniques. The soul must open its eyes and recognize the only true God and him whom he has sent: Jesus Christ.

The missionary of Christ then finds himself, at every instant, in the depth of mystery. And no doubt, because grace does not destroy nature, he is searching incessantly with all the effort—a painful effort—of his intelligence ways by which the message of the Gospel can enter the intelligences of his contemporaries. He must look for and find the individual and collective laws of humanity to which God has the humility to submit. He must be haunted by the thought that through his fault a man of good will may not hear the evangelical message. But at the same time he knows that at every instant the conveying of the Message is infinitely beyond him. He is not the Master of the Mission. God alone, the Holy Spirit alone, is the Master of the Mission.

He must also know that the manifestation of the love of God—and that is the purpose of the entire Christian apostolate—is a work of life, and, like all life, it communicates itself by contagion to those whom we "evangelize." Supernatural, fraternal charity "manifests," in the true sense of the word, the love with which God loves us. It is by loving one another—in such a true and divine manner—that God will be revealed. Here the Christian apostolate is much less the result of resounding words than of the silent power of love, a love that cannot be doubted because it is true and because it expresses itself through the reality of the Cross.

"Remember, I am sending you out to be like sheep among wolves; you must be wary, then, as serpents, and yet innocent as doves" (Matt. 10.16). We must hear the instructions of our Lord to his disciples, which are like the charter of the missionary (Matt. 10.16; Luke 10.1–12). From them we learn the manner proper to the Christian mission. We must be poor: "without purse, or wallet, or shoes." By this we understand that the missionary of God has put his complete trust in God. He does not depend upon himself, "not upon persuasive language, devised by human wisdom" (I Cor. 2.4). But he depends intrepidly upon God. He must not doubt him: "Did you go in want of anything, when I sent you out without purse, or wallet or shoes? They told him, Nothing" (Luke 22.35). The missionary of the poor Christ thus proves his unselfishness: "Give as you have received the gift, without payment" (Matt. 10.8).

Sent to evangelize the poor (Luke 7.22), how could he fail to be poor and share to some extent the life of the poor? Sent to announce Christ poor and crucified, how could he fail to be consumed by his message? Then "he gives no one greeting on his way" (Luke 10.4), not because he is indifferent, but in order not to stop. He will take rest after the light is kindled, and how far from it he

is! He will "go hungry and thirsty and naked; he will
be mishandled, have no home to settle in, hard put to it,
working with his own hands. Men will revile him, he
will be the world's refuse" (I Cor. 4.11–13). And yet, he
must continue to believe in Love. His arms will be but
truth and love: "You must be wary, then, as serpents, and
yet innocent as doves" (Matt. 10.16). Amazing words of
our Lord! Amidst a redoubtable world we shall never be
prudent enough, with the virile prudence of the adult and
strong man. And at the same time we must be simple as
doves, innocent and candid, disarming through a candor
that is not naïve. Who can avoid seeing here a miracle of
the Gospel?

These poor men will be brothers. Fraternal love will be
the sign by which the world will recognize that Christ is
truly sent by God (John 17.23). Vain glory, concern for
personal influence, jealous authority must be rejected. Only
one thing matters: that the Love of God be revealed. It is
the Kingdom of God that counts, not our own influence.

And finally patience will prevail: this profound patience
presented in the Scripture as the fruit of humility, of hope
and of love. We may experience agony. Our soul may be,
at times, plunged in sadness. The evil of the world is too
great, too heavy to bear by ourselves. But we shall look at
Christ on the Cross. We shall resemble him a little. And
he will simply say: "Take courage, I have overcome the
world" (John 16.33).